Christianity
for Beginners

Ralph Milton

Abingdon Press

Nashville

CHRISTIANITY FOR BEGINNERS

Copyright © 1996 by Ralph Milton

Published in Canada by Northstone Publishing Inc.

First Abingdon Press edition 1998

This book is printed on recycled, acid-free, elemental-chlorine-free paper.

Library of Congress Cataloging-in-Publication Data

Milton, Ralph
    [Common sense Christianity]
    Christianity for beginners / Ralph Milton.
        p   .cm.
    Originally published: Common sense Christianity.
Winfield. B.C. :
Wood Lake Books, [1988]
    Includes bibliographical references.
    ISBN 0-687-03469-8 (pbk : alk. paper)
    1. Theology, Doctrinal–Popular works.   I. Title.
BT77.M574   1998
230–dc21   97-50248
                                                              CIP

98 99 00 01 02 03 04 05 06 07 — 10 9 8 7 6 5 4 3 2

MANUFACTURED IN THE UNITED STATES
OF AMERICA

To Jim

Contents

Foreword 7

1. Don't Bother Me with Religion . . . 11

2. Religion vs. Science. 43

3. Who Is Jesus? 73

4. The Bible. 117

5. About God. 155

6. The Church 166

Postscript: Is It True?. 200

Recommended Reading. 206

Foreword

It was an interesting exercise going back and reading something I wrote more than eight years ago. My response to my own writing varied from delight to despair. But for the most part, I was convinced then and am convinced now that this book is a useful tool for those who want to get a good first overview of the Christian faith.

A number of things have changed: there have been subtle shifts in our public perception of the Christian faith and the churches—there's more emphasis on interfaith dialogue, a stronger realization within the churches that Christians are in many ways a minority faith. So I reworked the manuscript almost totally at several points, and generally polished and brought it up to date throughout.

The original manuscript was looked at and fussed over by some of the best minds in the various denominations. I won't name them, because that would imply they endorsed everything that's in the book, which is untrue.

But we did work together to produce a book that would be a fair and popular representation of the Christian Church, at least the churches that work together through what is generally known as the "ecumenical movement."

To those people, my deepest thanks.

Writing and rewriting this book has been a very helpful exercise. Trying to boil my convictions down to basics that can be expressed in clear, everyday language, meant I did a fair bit of pruning of the usual long-winded expression I give to my faith. It's amazing how the theological and traditional undergrowth obscures the trunk and the main branches. It's refreshing to let in a bit of light and air.

Living as I do in an agricultural area where I can see thousands of apple trees within a few hundred yards of my house, and having had my own small orchard, I know how important vigorous pruning is to healthy fruit.

I recommend it.

The first edition of this book, published by Wood Lake Books, proved to be a useful resource for people who wanted to know about the Christian faith, but who had no previous religious background. These people didn't want to be "converted." They wanted to be informed. Their feedback has been appreciated and a number of changes have improved the present volume as a result. I trust this new edition will be equally useful to as many folk.

One of the most moving accounts of the use of the first edition came from a woman (a theological librarian by profession) who volunteered at a drop-in center for street people (mostly prostitutes) in the city core. She left a copy of the book on the coffee table at the center. A few days later she noticed that the women were reading the book to each other, chapter by chapter. Over the course of a week these wounded women had read the entire book outloud to each other. For a writer, there is no greater reward than that kind of story.

A reading list at the back will, I hope, provide additional resources if this book raises more questions than it answers.

Which is exactly what I hope it will do.

R.M.
Kelowna, B.C., 1995

—1—

Don't Bother Me with Religion

If one of those polling companies asked you, you'd probably call yourself a Christian. Most North Americans do. No just *most*—a huge *majority* call themselves Christian. Anywhere between 75 percent and 95 percent of us claim to be Christian.

Reminds me of the Roadrunner. Last Saturday morning, I was channel surfing. I saw some Roadrunner cartoons—the same cartoons I had watched on black 'n' white TV with my kids—the same cartoons I had seen as a kid in the local theater back in the 1940s. Some things just keep going on forever.

The popular media have been convinced for years that Christianity was dead and gone and that except for a few doddery old folks and weird eccentrics, nobody believed it anymore.

Then somebody did a survey. Surprise! The roadrunner is honking and zooming across the screen while the media coyotes scratch their collective heads.

You can check any one of dozens of polls in Canada and the USA. They all agree. Most of us describe ourselves as Christian. We may not go to church, but we think of ourselves as Christian.

Some of us would really like to know what being "Christian" means. That's what this book is about. It's a description, not a sermon. So don't get nervous. Nobody is going to try to convert you.

Nor is this book a defense of Christianity. There are wild, weird, and downright dirty things attached to the word *Christianity,* and they will be just as wild, weird, and dirty when you've finished with this book.

There are people in the "religion business" for the money or the power. Their motivations aren't any more religious than those of people going into politics or the stock market. And some of the on- and off-screen antics of the TV evangelists could give "motherhood and apple pie" a bad name. Guilty as charged.

On the other hand, there is far more that is good and beautiful and constructive that has been done in the name of Christianity. But that part of the story hardly gets told because there's no kinky sex or greasy intrigue or brain-numbing violence. So the talk shows and the tabloids pay no attention.

If you are a "book-a-holic" like me, you'll know there are a bunch of recent books that offer new perspectives on religion. Some of them are very helpful, because they look at the various religious traditions and try to find the parts that are still helpful and useful—then build on that. Some of them, however, claim that nothing about traditional Christianity was ever good—that it was sexist, hierarchical, militaristic, racist, etc., and then go on to offer their particular solution. That is simply arrogant and destructive.

Christianity, like every other religious tradition, deserves much of the criticism it gets. There's lots that needs changing. But Christianity, like every other religious tradition, is also a gold-mine of insight and beauty and truth. There's lots that needs saving.

People who tell the pollsters they are Christian sense that, I think. Many of them would like to dust off the traditions of this ancient religion because they know it can give their lives beauty and meaning. If you are one of those, this book may be a good starting place for you.

Church

There's another part of the story the media have missed. Church. Does anybody still go? Another surprise. Again, the pollsters' figures vary depending on the region and the questions asked, but between 20 percent and 40 percent claim to go *regularly*. Yes, that is down a lot from what it used to be, but there still isn't a single TV network or national periodical that consistently reaches 20 percent of the population. If you added up all the local and national assets of any of the major denominations, they would be bigger than most of the multinational corporations. If you want to check it out, look under "churches" in the yellow pages of your phone book.

For several years, there's been a send-up piece circulating on the *Internet* and via photocopy machines to the effect that Microsoft Inc. had taken over the Vatican and made the Pope a vice president. It got to the point where enough people took it seriously that Microsoft had to issue an official denial. I laughed at the piece like everyone else, but the *Internet* clowns had the thing upside down. It's the Roman Catholic Church that would take over Microsoft. If you add up the worldwide assets of the Roman Catholic Church, Microsoft would look like small potatoes by comparison.

Don't count out the churches. Like the Roadrunner, when you are sure they are down and out, they honk a couple of times and zoom across your screen. The Christian faith, and the churches where that faith is celebrated, are alive and well and living in North America. Unlike most Europeans, Americans and Canadians are incurably religious, and insist on calling themselves Christian. So read on.

What Is Religion?

Religion "is the opium of the people," said Karl Marx, a famous atheist and the founder of the Communist party. He was right.

A young woman I know calls religion "a crutch for mental cripples." She's right too.

But so was D. T. Niles, a famous Christian from India, who said that telling the Christian story is like "one hungry beggar showing another hungry beggar where to find bread."

Teilhard de Chardin, the French philosopher, said that if once again the world discovers the power of love, then for the second time, humanity will have discovered fire.

All of them are right. Religion, including Christianity, has been and is being used as a drug to keep people away from real life. Religion is also a door through which many others find life. Religious faith is not a simple little formula you either buy or reject. Like anything else, it can be used and abused.

The Christian and Jewish faiths have affected every fiber of our western European culture. But we don't talk about it much in our schools, and you'll never hear much about it on *Oprah* or *Donahue.*

Yet, most of us think of ourselves as belonging to a religious group of some sort. If the pollsters ask us, we call ourselves Catholic, or United Methodist, or Jewish, or whatever. We want that church or synagogue or mosque to be there for special occasions such as marriages and funerals. But other than that, we don't think about our religious instincts very much. When religion does hit us in the face like the vaudevillian's cream pie, we react with surprise, even though we may be basically sympathetic.

My mom and dad considered themselves Christian, but they left the church they were raised in, and so I never saw the inside of a church till I went to my older sister's wedding. Religion got into the dinner table conversation once in awhile, but I didn't think much about it till I was an adult.

Nor have I had any dramatic religious experiences. In fact, for a number of years I was a DJ at a radio station where we carried evangelical programs wall-to-wall on Sundays. I sat through dozens of them, and not one of them got through to me.

Like most of the people I meet in my work as a writer, I had no religious background, but I was curious about religion. I wanted to know what it was about, but I was a bit nervous about getting hooked into something weird. Like most of us, I've been put off by sect groups ringing my doorbell, or by some of the TV evangelists.

But I'm a writer by trade. I'm trained to sniff out a lead and find the story. So I checked out this Christianity business and got really interested. Convinced. And yes, I now would call myself a Christian. That means I've lost my "objectivity" though I have never yet read any account of anything religious that was objective. Every reporter starts with some point of view and it always shows.

But I remember very well what it was like trying to satisfy my curiosity about Christianity, without having someone start preaching at me. I'll do my best to keep my personal convictions out of this, though nobody can be totally neutral. Please keep your mind open, read the book and then decide later whether to walk away from the whole business, or dig a little further. I'll try really hard to stay away from churchly jargon and I will do my best *not* to persuade you one way or another.

It's Good for the Kids

I have a couple of friends named Gary Simpson and Shawna Hubbard.

Shawna and Gary don't belong to any church. In fact, when it comes to discussions about religion, they can be quite eloquent about "superstition" and the "juvenile" idea of God.

Shawna and Gary are young and upwardly mobile. (You could call them "yuppies" but not to their face.) They both work. After they'd lived together for two years, Shawna got pregnant and they decided to get married because they felt it would be "better for the baby."

They got married in a church, even though "we don't believe in any of that stuff, really." But the fading legacy of Christianity they inherited from their parents is still there, sometimes. Especially at night, just before sleep, when they talk about the baby, and wonder what kind of a person that child might grow up to be. What they read in the papers bothers them; they worry about the violence in our society and about the quality of our political leadership. Sometimes they wonder if there isn't a better way of living than the dog-eat-dog atmosphere they see so much of.

Gary once found himself flipping through the pages of the Bible his grandmother had given them as a wedding present. This was after a conversation over coffee at the office when he'd said something about not believing in God anymore.

"What kind of God don't you believe in?" one of the secretaries asked.

"Well, you know," said Gary. "Some old man up there who zaps people if they don't flatter him enough."

"I don't believe in that kind of a God either," she said.

Gary didn't know what to say to that, and it bugged him. So he got down the Bible, even though he put it away quickly when he heard Shawna coming in the door.

And Shawna had found herself talking with a friend about the baby's baptism, and later wondered "why, for heaven's sake."

It never even occurred to Shawna and Gary that they might go to church on a Sunday. But when the census takers came around, they both filled in the denomination their parents had belonged to.

Gary and Shawna often get together with Andrew, a friend from Shawna's office. Andrew is very skilled at putting down anything religious. Sometimes he can be quite funny doing it.

"Christianity is simply an intellectual curiosity for me," says Andrew. "Those well-meaning Christians are nothing but Quixotes, carrying on an obsolete code of honor in rusty armor on a collapsing nag, with a mad and sadly comic energy." Under pressure, Andrew admits he stole the line from novelist Herman Wouk, who was actually writing about how some people thought about his own Jewish faith.

And yet Gary and Shawna did have the baby baptized. Andrew was there in church for the baptism, out of friendship for Gary and Shawna, nothing more. But he felt tears in his eyes when he heard the ancient benediction: "May the Lord bless you and keep you . . ."

Gary and Shawna are like thousands of other people who have no connection with the church any more, and who don't really think they are missing anything. But they often decide to get married in a church, to have their babies baptized, and then to take their kids to Sunday school because "it's good for the kids." Gary and Shawna are certainly not "religious," but they are not ready to give up on "religion."

Deep and Basic Instincts

You could call Shawna and Gary's feelings sniffly nosed sentimentality. Nostalgia maybe.

But if you scrape away the soft, sentimental sludge our society has layered over religious rites such as baptisms, weddings and funerals, you find a deep, visceral yearning for something more. Something real.

When you push Rudolph and the Little Drummer Boy out of the Christmas manger and chase the chocolate bunnies out of Jesus' grave, you find the heart of Christmas and of Easter beating, beating strongly, even though it's hard to hear over the traffic and the loudspeakers.

Popular culture either ignores religion or trivializes it. You could watch a year's worth of prime time TV and never hear religion of any kind even mentioned. Popular culture has substituted another kind of "religion" (though that term is never used): one which tells us we can achieve ultimate happiness by going for "the real thing" (Coke), or "the high life" (Miller) or any number of products that promise a kind of candy-coated answer to all of life's problems.

After another evening of TV commercials and newspaper ads telling them how to achieve instant happiness and popularity by buying more and more consumer goods, Gary and Shawna got to wondering. They found themselves reacting against things like the beer ad. "You only go around this life once, so you've got to grab all the gusto you can get."

As Shawna put it, "When we'd grabbed all that gusto, there we were—bleary eyed and hung over. All we had to show for it was a fat booze bill and a bulging 'Molson muscle.' We couldn't help wondering, 'Is that all there is?' "

For lack of a better phrase, call Shawna's question the "religious instinct." That instinct is part of our human nature. We can ignore it or repress it, and we may go to our graves not realizing we've got it. But the need, the instinct, is there. You can get only so much satisfaction out of "trivial pursuit," and then you start wondering about the hard questions. Maybe that's why you're reading this book.

Harold Kushner (an American rabbi who writes marvelous books such as *When Bad Things Happen to Good People*) tells of a young man who ran away from his middle-class home and joined the Unification Church. When they asked him why he joined the "Moonies," he said, "My father only talks about going to college and getting a good job. Reverend Moon talks to me about helping him save the world."

The young man wanted his life to matter. He wanted to count for something important.

That yearning is certainly not limited to young people. The world-famous psychiatrist, C. G. Jung, said that for his patients who were 35 years or older, the main problem was finding a religious outlook on life. "It is safe to say that every one of them fell ill because he had lost that which the living religions of every age have given their followers, and none of them has really been healed who did not regain his religious outlook."

Not long ago, a middle-aged friend was telling me about the death of a man he'd shared an office with for five years. "That could've been me!" he said several times. "I mean, I could drop dead any minute, just like him. He was even healthier than me. And already they've replaced him at the office. It's like he was never there. I mean, a guy's life should mean more than that, shouldn't it? Like, I could die anytime, and a couple of days later, they wouldn't even know I'd been here!"

People reaching retirement age start asking the question. One elderly gentleman told me he was "cramming for the finals."

I believe there are all sorts of people of various ages who come to some point in their lives when they want to know a little about that beautiful and frightening thing called "religion."

They want their lives to mean something.

Or they start searching because they're just plain scared.

Let's Get Personal

As a writer, I meet all kinds of people. Most of them don't call themselves "religious," much less "Christian." But I'm amazed at how many religious questions they ask. When they realize I can talk about Christianity without trying to lay a religious trip on them, they sometimes get pretty specific in their questions. They're hungry.

In the last few years, it's become common to say, "I'm a spiritual person, but I'm not religious." I think that translates as, "I believe there is a spiritual dimension to life, that there is a 'higher power,' but I am not connected to any church."

It is possible to be a "spiritual Christian," not connected to any church or community of faith, but it is very difficult. As I'll explain in more detail later, the essence of Christianity is the concept of *love,* and for love to happen there has to be more than one person. Whenever you get two or more people together who sense there is something spiritual about their relationship, you have what Christians call a church.

Organized Religion

Lots of people have been put off by organized religion, sometimes for very good reasons. My father had a running argument with his church all his life, and I was deeply affected by that.

When Bev and I were first married, I considered myself an atheist. And I could argue just as eloquently as our skeptical friend Andrew about the idiocy of religion in general and organized religion in particular. The excesses, the mindlessness, of some religious groups still burn me up.

The story of how I wound up becoming a religious person is told in boring detail in other books, so I won't repeat it here. But the root of my "conversion" was a niggling sense in the back of my head that once in awhile had me thinking, "Listen, turkey! You think you've got it all figured. You're great on logic, but your logic is telling you life is a meaningless accident. So don't give up on life. Give up on logic. There's a whole bunch you don't understand. Some things you're just going to have to believe."

Living through some tough and some beautiful times convinced me of three things.

- There's more to life than can be weighed or measured.
- There's a world of mystery, things we don't understand, in spite of all science has discovered.
- This mystery is not something vague or woolly or threatening, but something we encounter every day if only we have the wit to notice.

Psychiatrist Scott Peck, in his best-selling book *A Different Drum,* says we can only explain those things which are smaller than we are. Peck talks about a space heater in his office. An electrical engineer can explain the construction and wiring of the space heater. Anyone can observe what the electricity does. But no one has ever fully explained electricity itself. No one is ever likely to. Electricity is bigger than we are. Like so many of the really big things in life, it remains fundamentally a mystery.

Most of us have had religious experiences, even if we don't call them that—beautiful and enriching experiences which have been suppressed by an educational system that concentrates on teaching people how to earn a living rather than how to live.

Edward Robinson, in his book *The Original Vision,* describes his extensive research into childhood religious experiences, and has come to the conclusion that most of us have had such experiences.

I know I have. As a small boy I was told that the mother of one of my friends had shot herself. My own mother held me very close on her lap for a long, long time while I cried. I remember that moment with absolute clarity, even though I was only eight or nine years old.

I remember knowing at that moment, "God must be like my mom." You can see all kinds of social and psychological elements in that memory, that experience. But I'm convinced there was also something deeply religious about it.

Robinson's book is full of such stories. He says that most religious experiences, whether of adults or children, are not the kind of thing you hear about on religious talk shows on TV. Those spectacular "conversions" from a life of sin and crime may be real, but they're pretty far removed from our daily experience. Most of us have never been world-class crooks or mass murderers. Our "sins" are pretty ordinary. And "born-again" fever isn't something we can really relate to.

For most people, the religious experience is really something quite ordinary—even commonplace. It may be the birth of a child. Or a sunset. Or the sense that a loved one who has died is somehow still present with us. "What counts," says Robinson, "is neither the thunder nor the fire but the still small voice."

These religious experiences are by no means limited to Christianity. The Muslim faith has seen a worldwide revival. In our own country, aboriginal people have been rediscovering the spirituality that was so often discounted by the early missionaries. There's a renewed interest in dreams and their symbolic and religious significance. For a little while, angels were big. And of course, "new age" religion is growing, though it is sometimes very hard to say where "new age" begins and where Christianity leaves off. But that's another book.

I've never met a person who hasn't had some kind of experience they would call "religious." We tend to shrug off those experiences. I think we lose something important when we throw those experiences away. Those events, those insights, are small diamonds. The diamonds may be covered by dirt, but they're still diamonds. Many people assume the sparkle they see beside the road is really just a bit of broken glass, so they ignore it, or kick it into the ditch.

But life is tough, and we need those tiny diamonds—even if they are not the crown jewels. Even if they turn out to be just hunks of glass, they are still pretty. They can bring color and beauty into our lives, if we clean them and hold them up to the light.

The War Is Over

I wrote this book because I have a hunch our "civilization" has come to a turning point. I've heard it called the "post-scientific era."

I'm not really sure what that means, but let's play with the idea for a few paragraphs.

If this is the "post-scientific era" then it must come after the "scientific era." And before that we must have had a "pre-scientific era." Sounds profound anyway.

As our civilization moved from the pre-scientific era to the scientific era, there was a bloody, worldwide battle between religion and science. The battle was fought over many issues, especially the stories of how God created the world, which are told in the first few pages of the Bible, the part we call Genesis. Scientists and theologians had a merry old time sniping at each other over the question of whether the world was created in six days or whether it evolved over several zillion eons.

Now that war is pretty well over (except for a few diehard guerrilla groups fighting forgotten battles with tin soldiers). The guns rust in the fields and the grass slowly covers the graves.

The scientists won. At least, that's the way the history books tell the story. And so the scientists went about their work thinking the Bible and the religions it inspired would quietly die.

But Christianity didn't die. Nor did the other world religions. Even though there were lots of casualties in the battle, some real good came out of it, even for Christians. In the process, we learned a whole lot more about the Bible, what it tries to tell us and how it does its telling. We learned to use science to study religion.

We learned a little about science too—about its enormous potential—and about its limitations. Now we're even learning to use religion to study science!

We've learned that science, in spite of all its bravado, doesn't have all the answers either. When all the marvels of interstellar matter and molecular mechanics are measured, and all the particulars of human plumbing have been penetrated, we're still left with the most ancient of all questions:

• "Who am I?"
• "Does my life have any meaning?"
• "What happens when I die?"

Which Religion?

So you feel the need for a religious expression to your life. Okay. Which religion are you going to choose? How do you go about making such a choice? The same way you'd make any other major choice in your life—by finding out as much as you can, then making a careful, rational decision.

Or you may do as I did—simply take an intuitive leap. I leaped into Christianity because it was my "home." Like most Europeans and Americans (both North and South) I was raised in a "Christian" culture, where I was familiar with the festivals (Christmas, Easter, Halloween, Thanksgiving, and so on), where the legal system is based on the Judeo-Christian tradition, and where our literature and culture is redolent with Christian symbols.

So why not just affirm the goodness and the equality of all the world's great religions? Don't they all believe and teach the same basic things?

Only if you have a very simple mind, and you never look beyond the superficialities.

Madonna (the singer) and Mother Teresa both talk a lot about love, but they mean very different things. The various religions use many of the same terms and symbols, but once you get beyond superficialities, they are very different.

Which does not mean that because Christianity is my religion, I think other religions are wrong. In fact, the more I know about my own faith and the richness of the Christian tradition, the more I can appreciate other faith traditions and learn from them.

I've always enjoyed good food, but when I learned a bit about cooking, I was able to really enjoy and discuss the foods served to me by friends.

I'm not going to answer those questions for you, mostly because you and I each have to find the answers for ourselves. But I will try to give you a "Cook's Tour" of a religion called Christianity, which for two thousand years has been trying to help people find answers to those questions. Sometimes it succeeded.

The Bible Put Me to Sleep

I never went to church as a kid. My mom and dad had reacted pretty negatively to the narrow-minded church of their time, so they just stayed away. When that "religious question" started bubbling in the back of my brain, I found myself both fascinated and confused by Christianity. Like anything unfamiliar, I viewed it with suspicion. So I avoided religion as much as I could.

Yet deep down, I knew there was something important in all that gobbledygook, something that could make a big difference to my life. I sensed a beautiful mystery.

There were incidents like the one with my mom. I knew I hadn't sorted them out and that somehow I wanted to. Christians, I figured, must know about these things.

So I asked friends who went to church regularly, "What do you believe, anyway?"

"We believe in Jesus," they said, as if they had memorized the answer. They probably had.

"Who is this guy Jesus?" I asked.

"Jesus was God incarnate."

Now what was that supposed to mean?

I knew there was a book called the Bible, though I hadn't actually read any of it. I knew the Bible was about God and Jesus and that sort of thing. The Bible, I assumed, talked about God being "up there," and somebody called Jesus who at one point had been "down here," but beyond that, I couldn't have told you much about it.

Once I even sat down to read the Bible. What I read was pretty confusing and in an archaic form of English full of "thee's" and "thou's" that sounded a lot like Shakespeare. Mostly, it put me to sleep.

I wasn't even sure what a "Christian" was, except that Christians went to church. I had no idea what happened in their church, though I suspected they were mostly told what *not* to do. I had seen a poster once that said, "Everything I like is either indecent, immoral, or fattening." I figured Christianity must be like that.

I remembered a girl I went out with a couple of times when I was a teenager. One day, when I tried to take her hand as we walked home from school, she said, "No, I'm a Christian." At the time, I couldn't figure out why being a "Christian" meant she couldn't hold my hand. I still can't.

Not a Snow Job

I started looking around for something to read, something written for reasonably intelligent adults who had not been raised in a Christian church, but who would like to find out a bit more about what Christianity is and does and teaches. I couldn't find anything. I couldn't find anything that wasn't trying to convert me.

Several decades later, I still can't find anything that starts at square one and doesn't try to talk me into something.

So I'm not really writing this book for you. I'm writing this book for myself. Nobody learns as much from a book as the one who writes it.

I promise to describe Christianity as honestly and openly as I know how. I'll try not to pull my punches when we get to some of the excesses, eccentricities, and sometimes downright dishonesty of people who call themselves Christian. The story of the Christian faith is not all sweetness and light.

But every writer has a bias. If I were an atheist writing about Christianity, I'd reflect an anti-Christian bias.

There's no such thing as an "independent" and "impartial" description of anything. I learned that during my years as a news reporter. I would cover an event or a meeting along with other reporters. Each one of our news stories picked up slightly different flavors of what happened, emphasized different things, and reflected different biases.

To get a balanced perspective on anything, it's good to read several different accounts, each told from a different perspective. So I certainly hope this isn't the only book you read on Christianity.

My bias will become pretty evident as you read, so I might as well come clean right now. I am head over heels in love with my God and with the people in God's church. While I'm not consciously going to try and talk you into anything, you will have to take my biases into consideration as you read.

One thing is for sure. Not every Christian will agree with my description of the faith. In fact, what follows will make some very religious people absolutely livid. That's okay. My recommendation is that you listen to them too, if you can, and make up your own mind.

Just don't take my word as the final answer to anything. This book will give you the basis to dig further into the Christian story, assuming I don't totally turn you off in the process. I think you'll discover as I did, that religion in general, and Christianity in particular, are fascinating, whether you wind up believing any of it or not. The Christian tradition is full of rich ideas and profound insights and a fair bit of fun.

Speaking of fun—there have been Christians who looked down their long noses and said, "Thou shalt not laugh!" There aren't too many of those kind around anymore. I'm not sorry. Personally, I couldn't hang onto a religion that didn't offer me a good belly laugh now and again.

Laughing about something doesn't mean a put-down. I laugh with and about my kids, my wife, and my friends. I love them all, and my laughter is one expression of that love. In the same way I laugh about my church and about my Christian faith. My laughter is one expression of that love.

Have fun!

—2—

Religion vs. Science

Let's not mess around. Let's go right to the heart of the matter and talk about God—and the phony war between God and science.

Just about everybody believes in a god of some kind. I don't suppose there are any worldwide surveys, but North American statistics show that genuine atheists—people who are absolutely sure there is no such thing as a "god"—make up no more than one or two percent of the whole population, if that.

It Starts in the Belly

So I won't try to prove that God exists. Far better brains than mine have been trying to do that for centuries. The best attempt was by Thomas Aquinas, an Italian who lived in the 13th century. He almost had a cerebral hernia trying to prove, logically, that God existed. Any good encyclopedia will give you a summary of his arguments. But the judgment of history has been, "Close, Tom. But no cigar."

In the last few years, something interesting has appeared on the scientific horizon. In fields such as mathematics, quantum physics, biology and medicine, as research scientists push back the far horizons of knowledge, they're finding themselves considering questions that sound more like religion than science. At the far end of all the equations and hypotheses, scientists find themselves probing questions of meaning and purpose, of design and relationship. Theologians might say that scientists sometimes see the face of God.

Not all scientists of course. But some of our best scientific brains have been in the heads of very religious people. Albert Einstein, for instance, who said, "Science without religion is lame. Religion without science is blind."

Einstein was Jewish and I've dragged him into a book about Christianity, but the basic assumptions of the major world religions are very similar. I'm sure Einstein would agree with the categorical statement I'm going to make right now.

There is no conflict between scientific truth and religious truth.

None. Zip.

We get at some kinds of truth through scientific method, and at other kinds of truth through hunches, feelings, metaphors, images and the arts. And through our religious faith.

A scientist can tell you how the refraction of light in droplets of water causes rainbows, but a poet can write a song about the beauty of rainbows. One truth about rainbows doesn't deny the other truth.

Sometimes, when I want to make that point with children, I ask one of them to stand and look at me from the front and another to look at me from the back.

"What do you see?" I ask the child at the front.

"A big nose!" said one young observer.

Then I ask the child behind me . . .

"A bald spot."

"Both of you are right. But because you are looking at me from different angles, you see different things." Science and religion see reality from different angles—different perspectives. When they come up with different observations, it is not because one of them is wrong, but because they are looking at different kinds of evidence.

The conflict is not between science and religion, but between people who are insecure because they (and the rest of the human race) know so very little about either science *or* religion. So they yell and scream and get into fights.

If proving things scientifically turns you on, you're reading the wrong book. I can't prove the existence of God or much of anything else about religion with the scientific method. I'm simply going to rest my case on the fact that just as human beings in every part of the world and through centuries of time have gazed in awe at rainbows and known they are beautiful, so most human beings know there is a force or a being that is somehow involved in our lives.

Just about everybody everywhere believes in some kind of "god." They might believe in anything from an abstract "life force" to "ultimate reality," to an angry grandfather in the sky who will zap you if you notice a good-looking body of the opposite sex. They all agree there is some "power" larger than they are.

Instead of trying to prove the existence of God, which I can't do anyway, let's talk about the things that lead people to an awareness of God in the first place. That awareness can start in the belly or the brain. Or both.

Terrifying and Thrilling

For me, it started in the belly. With my feelings. My brain had been telling me for years there was no such thing as a god. During my late teens when I knew everything, I told anyone who would listen that I was an atheist. On the odd occasion when my belly seemed to argue with my brain, I put it down to the greasy food "Ma" Addison fed us at her boarding-house.

Then I met a very special woman and discovered the mystery of love. Together Bev and I had children. "Something fantastic is going on here," a voice without words seemed to be saying inside me. "What's it all about?"

That's the basic question, isn't it? "What's it all about?" "How do I make sense of life?" "How do I make sense of the world?" "Why am I here?" And searching for the mystery of it all can be terrifying or thrilling. Probably both.

It's the terror and the thrill of life, the need to make sense of all the things that happen, which leads humans to begin the search for ultimate meaning. For God.

Umpteen zillion years ago, our great, great, great grandparents sat on a rock somewhere, picking lice out of each other's hair and wondering. They saw the moon and the stars. They ran into their caves to hide from the thunder. Life was short and brutish. Gradually the idea of a god began to form in their imagination; or more correctly, the idea of many gods.

"The lightning must be alive because it moves," they said. "It speaks and kills. The sun must be alive too, and the same thing with the moon and the stars and the trees and the river."

Or, as one goldfish said to another, "If there's no god, then who changes the water every week?"

The idea of gods, beings who were greater and more powerful than humans, beings that lived in rocks and trees and animals and clouds, emerged over the centuries of early human development. The earliest artifacts from the first, most primitive humans show they had elaborate beliefs in gods and spirits.

The stories, the legends, grew and developed for the same reason that people do scientific research today. The myths and legends helped our ancestors explain how the world worked. They had stumbled upon a basic philosophical idea: that things and events and people have meaning. It is this kind of wondering that gave rise to all the world's religions.

Our primitive ancestors wanted to understand the meaning of their lives, but even more important, they wanted to be able to control things a bit. So they developed ritual and song and dance and all sorts of incantations as ways of bribing or flattering or fooling those gods and spirits so that events would turn out better for them. Our ancestors' motives were much the same as ours.

"Things go better when you bribe the spirits with an animal sacrifice," our forebears said. "Things go better with Coke," we say. You tell me which incantation makes more sense.

Eventually the revolutionary idea began to dawn on our spiritual ancestors, the idea that maybe there weren't a whole bunch of gods. Maybe there was just one god. The God.

Hey Dimwit! Pay Attention!

I could go on tracing the development of religious thought and practice the way they do in comparative religion courses at the universities. But from my perspective as a Christian, I've got to make a statement that is the key to everything else that follows in this book.

Our spiritual ancestors discovered that God wasn't sitting up on a cloud somewhere watching it all happen. Nor was God, or the gods, playing games with us.

God was right in there helping it happen because (and this is the radical part) God loved us. And still does. It takes a huge leap of the imagination, or a huge leap of faith to believe that one. It's not something Christians can prove in any way. We believe it because it matches our experience.

When I stood in the hospital as a young man holding a new baby in my arms, and feeling—more than thinking—those huge universal questions, that was God tickling me with a gentle feather and saying, "Hey, dimwit! Pay attention. You can learn something."

And when my ancestors stood on that rock and stared wide-eyed at the lightning, God was prodding their primitive minds with a new awareness of something holy.

I have to get even more specific. Those ancestors came to feel that though this God was the creator of everything and everybody, this God had a very particular interest in an insignificant, nondescript tribe of people in the Middle East known as the Hebrews.

I belong to what social scientists call the Judeo-Christian tradition. My spiritual ancestors in that tradition came to a very specific kind of conclusion. They believed that the "bigger, more powerful something" is God. They called that ancient God "YHWH," or "Yahweh." Or, as some ancient versions of scripture incorrectly translated the word, "Jehovah." It's the same God whom Muslims call Allah.

God's involvement with those Hebrew people, the ancestors of modern day Jews—God trying to get through to them, lavishing love on them, trying to get them to love back, trying to help them be honest and decent and fair—that's the story in the Bible. (I'll talk about the Bible in chapter four.)

Christianity isn't just a set of things we believe, or a bunch of things we do. Christianity is also a history that goes back thousands of years, a history of God trying to help us understand that basic question: "What's it all about?" and "How can it possibly be that this God loves me?"

In other words, the questions you and I ask are not much different from the questions our ancestors asked, perched on a rock in the bush and watching the lightning flash. Our ancestors concluded that there was more to reality than could be seen with the eye, more than could be measured and touched. "There's a mystery about all this, and it's bigger and more powerful than me," was their conclusion.

A Bit Far-fetched

Now, centuries later, with all our scientific sophistication, we're still coming to the same conclusion: "There's a mystery about all this, and it's bigger and more powerful than me." We describe that conclusion in many different ways, but the conclusion itself is fundamental to everything we generally call "religion."

Amazing stuff really, when you put it down in that kind of a bald statement. Actually, it seems a bit far-fetched. It would be nice if we could prove that sort of statement, or at least make a good scientific case for it.

Nobody has ever proved (in the scientific sense) that God exists, much less that God loves us (as Christians, Muslims, Jews and other religions insist). Millions of very intelligent people believe it anyway. The belief isn't founded in proof. It's founded in personal experience.

No Proof

Here's how I understand it.

I am in love with Bev. I've been in love with her for 38 years at this writing. Most of the time at least.

I also believe firmly that Bev loves me back. Most of the time at least. Everything inside me says this is true.

But I couldn't possibly prove my love or hers.

I can tell you stories about our love, about the closeness we share, about the gifts we've given each other. That would be good circumstantial evidence, but you could rightly argue that it's only evidence. Not proof.

I could claim that 38 years together should count for something, and it does. But it doesn't prove anything. Husbands and wives have lived together for more years than that and not loved each other. Maybe Bev and I are just pathologically codependent.

Bev and I could say we've been sexually faithful to each other, but you might also argue that we've just been too chicken to cheat. Both of us would be partly right.

You'd be able to point out that our marriage has not been a rose-garden romance. Bev and I have had some pretty destructive fights. Our marriage has been close to coming apart on several occasions, and we've had to get professional help to rebuild our relationship.

When you and I get sick of bickering about this, I'd simply have to stand here flat-footed and maintain that I know Bev and I love each other. Every fiber in my body, every experience (good and bad) of our married life says it's true. Whether you accept or reject that statement, that evidence, is up to you.

Actually, I wouldn't expect you to believe me, unless you've had a similar experience of love. If you have, you'll know what I'm blathering about. If not, well, we don't have much in common to talk about.

A Believer's Bifocals

Here's another concept to help you get a handle on how Christians think and feel. When Bev and I read through old letters we've sent to each other, we understand meanings behind the words that you can never understand, unless you believe that two people can be deeply and honestly in love, and can stay that way through more than a few fights and four teenagers growing up.

You'll never know why a rather ordinary watercolor painting is so important to us, especially to Bev. But if we told you how that painting is the one keepsake Bev has from her Grandma Dill, how the painting was lost for five years and then "miraculously" found again, then you'd know why that painting is so valuable to us.

Or at least you'd understand if there are things you treasure for the same kinds of reasons. In the same way, you'll understand what we mean by religious experiences, if you'd had something you would also call a religious experience.

Every religion is based on experience. That's why people with strong religious convictions have such a hard time explaining themselves sometimes. Religions, all religions, ask us to think in a way that isn't always highly regarded in scientific or hard-nosed business circles. And most jaded newspaper and TV reporters and writers understand it not at all. No wonder religion gets such bad press!

We Christians read the Bible and other religious writings. All sorts of meanings leap out at us. We go to church and participate in a ritual that may seem rather silly to some people. But for Christians, that ritual is a breath of life.

That's because Christians are involved in a huge, universal love affair with God. When you're in love, you have a deep need to spend time with your beloved, to understand, to communicate. That's true when you're in love with another person. It's far more so when you're in love with God.

Christians often make the mistake of expecting people who are not in love with God to see the same meanings that we see. That's not fair. We see life through a particular kind of bifocal lens that sees not only the world everyone else sees, but another reality at the same time.

A very good friend of mine had a cat. He loved that cat. It had been part of his family for years.

My friend tolerated the cat when she threw up on his shoes, had kittens on his bed, and got too old and feeble to find her litter box in the middle of the night. Because he loved the cat, he couldn't understand how other people reacted with disgust or avoidance. They didn't love the cat. He did.

In the same way, we who are already Christians read those old stories in the Bible, we celebrate our faith through an ancient ritual, and the love of God seems to leap out at us. We think the meaning should be obvious to others, but of course it isn't.

Well-meaning Christians often try to prove their faith by quoting from the Bible. Their enthusiasm outruns their good sense. Proving Christianity by quoting the Bible is like proving I love Bev by quoting from one of my letters to her. Evidence it may be. Proof it ain't.

A Free Trip to Disney World

You should be getting a bit impatient by now. "So enough with this love business. What is God like?"

It would make my job so much easier if I could give you a description of God in 25 words or less. I can't. Please be patient. This human race of ours has been trying to sort out the God question since the first primitive person woke up one morning wondering why the sun rose every day.

Think of an unborn child. Not until the child moves from the world of the womb to another reality will the child see the face of its mother. We can't imagine the face of God either, though, like that unborn child, we try hard to do so. In our struggles, we've come up with quite a collection of concepts. Some are wild, some are pretty woolly, and a few are genuinely wonderful.

Here are a few of the most popular ideas about God. Some will probably make more sense to you than others, depending on what your experiences have been. Some will really turn you off. Or at least, they should.

Play a little game with yourself. Pick the one and only true description of God, and you win eternal happiness plus a free trip to Disney World.

- **God the General.** God sits "up there" in command headquarters, directing the troops down here on earth. If the infantry gets a bit outnumbered, General God can always bring in the air force (angels) to join in the battle. General God is always totally

on your side and against the "enemy," who-
ever the enemy happens to be that day.

- **God the Coach.** If you pay attention to the
signals from the bench, you'll win for sure.
But Coach God has scruples. If you don't
play by the rules you'll get benched. You
might even get kicked off the team.

- **God the Computer Hack.** This god
doesn't care at all what happens to us. Computer Hack God set up the world, worked
out all the programs, booted up the system,
typed in the "do" command, and then went
on to invent something else. It doesn't much
matter how many bugs the software has,
Computer Hack God is busy with other
things and really doesn't care.

- **God the Cop.** Here comes the fuzz! The
Constable God has your little computer
brain hot-wired into master control, and if
you press the wrong button or try to access
a protected file or get your pinkies into the
wrong cookie jar, "El-zappo!" God'll get you
for that!

- **God the Rock Star.** Some people think of God as a prima donna artist, a very popular, flamboyant Super Star who has lots of fans, lots of money, lots of connections, and above all, lots of ego. If you want to be part of it, you've got to be one of the groupies who follows the Star around saying flattering things, giving the Star credit for everything good that happens, and taking responsibility yourself for everything bad. When you're "in" with the Star, you've got it made.

  A variation of this is the Superhero God, who will fly in and zap the bad guys, do marvelous miracles for the fans, and make you feel good all over.

- **God the Kindergarten Teacher.** As long as you're in school, Kindergarten Teacher God will feed you cookies, wipe your runny nose and give you a hug when you cry. This God will also help you put on dry clothes if you mess your pants. But once you leave kindergarten you're on your own.

- **God the Social Worker.** God is very help-ful, but only in the sense of giving really good advice. You still have to make your own decisions and take responsibility for them. And the Social Worker God is ready to talk to anyone needing a bit of advice.

A variation of this is the idea of God as "best friend," someone who is with you all the time, who provides moral support when you're feeling down and goes for long walks with you when you're depressed.

- **God the Parent.** God is a very good, very caring Parent. The Parent God, traditionally referred to as Father but sometimes also as Mother, is loving and tender, and has read all the books on how to raise children to be mature and responsible adults. Parent God hurts when the kids mess up. But even so, Parent God knows that's the only way for the kids to grow. They've got to have the freedom. Totally. The Parent God respects us, and believes passionately that we can and will grow up. This Parent God gets really upset when the kids fight with each other, or refuse to share things with each other.

- **God the Lover.** Like the Parent God in many ways, Lover God has read all the human potential literature, and wants us to be totally free to love back. So Lover God is never manipulative or bossy. There's always a shoulder to cry on, and when you ask, Lover God will be ready to go to bat for you. There are a bunch of Christian songs written about the Lover God, and yes, they are slightly erotic, which isn't necessarily bad.

- **God the Artist.** God loves to make beautiful things—trees and ducks and people and worlds. The Artist God is wildly extravagant, using up the whole universe for a star-studded, microbe-punctuated gallery. It's a living art exhibit, and the show keeps changing. God has appointed the human race as the curator of this magnificent gallery. We're asked to look after it, to keep it neat and tidy, to love it and appreciate the intricate, delicate beauty of it all, and to make sure there's no vandalism.

So guess! Which is the right answer?

All of them. (Well, almost all.)

And none of them.

Because any one of them—even any two or three of them—is a distortion. Like a small child's perception of adults as mostly kneecaps and loud voices.

And even if you put all of them together, that wouldn't be right either, because there's more to God than any definition, just as there's more to you and to me than any description of us.

Nice try anyway. For your efforts, you may (I hope) find eternal happiness, but forget the trip to Disney World.

Missed by a Country Mile

Our problem is our pea-sized brains. We try to describe God in words and ideas that we understand, and that's impossible. No matter what we call God, or how we describe God, we flunk out because we don't have the words or the intelligence to do it.

Way back in the Middle Ages, an obscure monk wrote a little booklet in which he tried to list a thousand names for God. He went on and on. Creator, Redeemer, Shepherd, Friend, Judge, Counselor, King, Brother, Sister, Sustainer, Lord, Mother, Father, Eternal One, etc., etc., etc. And of course, any one of those names was partly right and partly wrong. All of them were incomplete.

On the other hand, maybe it's not so much our lack of intelligence as our inadequate language. We try to describe God in the same way we might describe the computer on which I'm writing this book; in very specific and non-fuzzy terms. I have a computer manual that gives me the "file names in the *Windows* operating system." Those files have exotic names such as "EXE2BIN.EXE" and "LLFDFMT.COM."

Each file name describes a small part of the reality of *Windows* or *MS-DOS* (whatever *MS-DOS* is). In somewhat the same way, the various names and descriptions for God describe one part of the reality of God. None of them tells you the whole thing. But there's a difference.

The names of God are metaphors. What's a metaphor. It's a marvelous device we humans have worked out in our language for putting labels on reality so that we can see beyond the obvious—for connecting two parts of reality so that, by joining them, we somehow know more about both of them.

It's one of the most common figures of speech. Your English teacher tried to explain this to you in High School. "He's a sly fox." "Watch Gretzky fly!" "The road was a ribbon of moonlight . . ."

This morning I told Bev I didn't feel like getting out of bed. "I have contracted a terminal case of torpor," I said to her.

Her response: "Get out of bed, turkey!"

My response: "You're a slave driver!"

I didn't mean that Bev was exactly like a slave driver, or that she always acts like a slave driver. I meant that one aspect of who she was at that particular moment, was like a slave driver. And I don't think Bev meant that in every respect and at all times I look or act like a turkey, but then . . .

Of course, metaphors are not the only figures of speech we use to help us understand the reality of our faith. Each figure of speech, each little bit of imagination we add to the language to help us describe the indescribable, shows us another bit of reality.

Each figure of speech is a snapshot that captures a small moment or a small part of reality, but seeing that moment helps us understand the whole so much better. We have many poetic ways of describing God. No one word or phrase is ever adequate, but each one helps us capture one part of the huge mysterious reality. Even the Bible uses a whole variety of different names and metaphors for God.

So we can call God a "universal cosmic force" at one moment and a "personal friend" at another. I often think of God as "Father," but I also think of God as "Mother." One doesn't exclude the other.

Exciting and Rich

Maybe we should send a photographer to heaven, or program a space probe to send back pictures. But we'd probably get closer to the truth if we go with the child who announced that she was going to draw a picture of God.

"But nobody knows what God looks like," protested her mother.

"They will now!" said the child.

So how can we get a handle on what God is about? That question takes us back around to what I was saying in the first place about how we experience God.

Thinking about what God is like, studying the arguments in favor and against the various positions, is a good idea. It helps clear up some fuzzy thinking that can really get in the way of knowing who or what God is.

Thinking and studying about God is what we call theology. The girl drawing the picture was doing theology. We all do theology once in a while. It can be very exciting and rich, a great banquet of ideas and insights.

What Is God Like?

One of the unique things about the Christian faith is that we say, "Forget trying to figure out with our human brains what God is like. None of us is smart enough for that." Of course, we don't always practice what we preach, so we do spend lots of energy trying to do the impossible.

Still when you strip away all the verbiage, the way Christians know what God is like is by knowing what Jesus is like. (Yes, I know I haven't told you who Jesus is. That's the next chapter.) God is an experience, and Christians claim they experience God in the person of Jesus of Nazareth.

Not exclusively, of course. Sometimes I see flashes of holiness in the people I meet and love. But when you get right down to it, when the question comes up about what God is like, we say, "Take a look at Jesus. Look at the kind of a person he was. Look at what he did. Listen to what he said. Then you'll sense a bit of what God is like."

That's what Christians mean when they say "Jesus is God incarnate": God in the flesh, in a human body, like ours.

To understand what Christianity is about, and what kind of God Christians worship, you have to get to know Jesus a little better.

For that matter, you can't really understand how Christians read the Bible until you know what Jesus was about.

That's why, before we get to talking about the Bible, we have a chapter on Jesus.

Just a Sniff

What you've read in this chapter is just a sniff drifting out of the kitchen where the cook is at work. If you'd like to look at the menu, read on. But keep in mind, it's a Christian menu. It is not the same as the Muslim menu down the road, or the Jewish menu next door, or the Buddhist or aboriginal menus. It is not even the same as the fundamentalist Christian menu. But the food in one shop is not better or worse than the food in any other. Simply different. Each of us, I think, needs to choose our own food to feed our soul.

This book is about basic mainline Christianity, both Protestant and Catholic, and represents my invitation to sample a meal of pretty standard "Christian soul food." But Christians are creative cooks, and there are a million wonderful variations on this theme. Please don't be satisfied with just this serving.

—3—

Who Is Jesus?

The Christian story begins today.

Before you think I've blown a mental fuse, let me explain.

My dad was about 50 when I was born, so the age difference between us was more than for most fathers and sons.

I used to see my father as a stuffy, old-fashioned reactionary. He died when I was in my early twenties, so I never got to know him after I'd finished my teenage rebellion.

In the years since he died, I've learned a bunch about my dad. Mom shared some old scrapbooks that he had kept. She told me stories I'd never heard or had forgotten. My older brother and sisters talk about him from time to time, and so, over the years, my feelings about Dad have changed.

Mostly, however, I've grown up a bit. My attitudes and my values have changed (for the better, I hope). And because I have experienced some of the things Dad experienced—such as being a father of teenagers—I see him in a totally different light. Some of the things that happened in my childhood take on a whole new meaning. Dad has been dead for 38 years, but I'm still learning about him.

So in that sense, the story of my father, at least *my* story of my father, begins with my awareness of who he was. My story about my dad didn't begin the day he was born, but when I began to get to know him as a real person. And that story keeps on growing as I learn more about him and about myself.

In the same way, the Christian story begins with our growing awareness of what being a Christian means. Then as we look back on the facts of history, we can understand them from that perspective.

The Center of the Story

The center of the Christian faith is Jesus. Take away Jesus, and you have no Christian faith.

Christianity comes in a bewildering variety of denominations and sects, but they all agree on that one central point.

And the story of Jesus begins right now. Today. Each time a person discovers the Christian faith, each time someone studies the Christian faith, believes the Christian faith, and acts out the Christian faith, the story of Jesus is enlarged and enriched, and becomes a brand new story.

That happens every day. We discover the newness and the vitality and the richness. Just when we think we have Jesus pegged, a new insight comes along and hits us right between the eyes.

Also, with advances in modern archaeology, with far better understanding of the original languages in which the Bible was written, with much more competent scholarship, we have better translations of the Bible and a far more detailed understanding of the life and times in which Jesus lived.

Exciting and Silly

The Christian faith is a living thing. With each living of that faith, the understanding grows and is enriched.

And like every living thing, it changes as it grows. Some people find that idea very threatening. It might be simpler if we could lock in on one set of ideas, one way of doing things, a set of clear rules. I frankly think it would be pretty boring. Anyway, nothing in human society, including the Christian faith, works that way.

When Bev and I were first married, we thought we had our relationship figured out. My job was to go out and conquer the world. Bev's job was to populate it.

That marriage relationship is far different now. The world has changed and so have we. Bev is now a highly respected professional. Love, commitment, a fair number of hassles, and professional help from caring people in our church, has tied us together all these years. But our relationship has changed. Mostly for the better.

Christianity, like a marriage, is a living relationship. It is not a collection of facts and dogmas. It's not a set of ideas or rules. Christianity is a community of people in a living relationship with God.

That living relationship has changed. Christianity today is not the same as it was in my parents' day, not even the same as it was ten years ago. It's dynamic. Some of the changes are for the better and some are not.

Just as love lives on through the changes in a marriage relationship, we believe that in some beautiful and mysterious way, the spirit of Jesus is still very much with us in a changing and dynamic Christian faith. That spirit in our lives, and in the life and work of our Christian community, helps us understand the story.

Begin at the Beginning

One of the names we use for Jesus is "Emmanuel," which means "God with us." The knowledge that God is with us in the spirit of Jesus is the beginning of our story. So, to tell you a bit about the story of Jesus, I have to begin with the point at which people first became aware that Jesus was not just a human being who lived and died at a particular point in history (though he was certainly that), but Emmanuel, God with us.

I think the story begins early on a Sunday morning. A small group of his followers were bringing some sweet-smelling spices to the grave of Jesus. They wanted to honor a friend who had been executed for treason. They came to mourn the loss of a great person and a fine leader.

When they arrived at the graveyard, Jesus' body was not in the tomb. It was gone. Most of the group, after shaking their heads and wondering about it all, went back home. But one of the group, a woman who'd had more than her share of problems in life, stayed behind to weep.

Her name was Mary of Magdala. And through her tears, Mary saw someone she thought at first was the groundskeeper. But when he spoke, Mary knew it was Jesus. She had no idea how this could be. She had seen Jesus dead. Now she was seeing him alive.

Jesus, alive in a new way, appeared a number of times to his followers. He talked with them, walked with them, and promised that even though he wouldn't be visible to them, he would be present. Always.

Mary and the others with her had discovered an empty grave. But it's not Jesus' absence from an empty tomb that puts the enthusiasm into the Christian community. It's his living presence in our lives.

And that presence is celebrated by Christians over and over. The first Easter happened on a Sunday. In a sense, Christians celebrate Easter every Sunday. That's why most Christians set aside Sunday as their special day.

A few years after his death, the followers of Jesus began putting the story down on paper in what we now know as the New Testament portion of the Bible. They had told each other the story many times, and heard it told by others.

Not everything written about Jesus made it into the Bible. For instance, there was an active group called the Gnostics who had a very different perspective on who Jesus was. That group didn't survive, and their writings were suppressed by the early Church. But they had some very interesting and creative ideas.

Because Christian groups were springing up in many places, the story had to be translated into other languages and cultures. As these early Christians lived and prayed their faith, a little light would go on in their heads. "Aha! Now I understand why Jesus did that!" Or, "That's why he said that!" And they wrote that understanding into the narrative.

At the same time, other parts of the story of Jesus were forgotten. Some details didn't seem important to the story and so they got dropped. For instance, nowhere do we have a description of what Jesus looked like. Much was lost, but on the other hand, each community in which the story was told added its own richness, its own living faith to the story.

If you believe the story, as millions do, it's pretty exciting stuff. If you don't, it must sound pretty silly.

The heart of the story of Jesus is Easter morning. The heart of the story is the Christian conviction that the love of God can break through the deepest evil humanity can imagine—that life is more powerful than death.

So, having said the story does not begin with the birth of Jesus, let's begin telling the story there anyway, simply to get it in the right sequence.

The First Christmas

Mary and Joseph lived in a little jerkwater town called Nazareth. Joseph was the village carpenter.

One day word came from the authorities that there was to be a census. It wasn't like today's census with someone knocking on the door and asking you questions about whether you have indoor plumbing and how many cars.

Joseph and Mary had to go to Bethlehem to be counted, because that was Joseph's hometown. It wasn't all that far by today's standards. But on foot, or maybe on a donkey, it was a fair hike. And Mary was eight and a half months pregnant. Not fun.

When Mary and Joseph got to Bethlehem, no one would give them a place to stay, so the baby wound up being born in a barn.

They named the baby "Jesus," a common name in those days (it still is in Spanish speaking areas). It means, "Yahweh (God) is salvation."

Angels appeared to a scraggly bunch of shepherds telling them about the birth, so they came to visit and to worship the baby. And they were followed by astrologers (usually called the three kings or three wise men, though the Bible doesn't tell us how many there were). The astrologers brought gifts of gold, frankincense, and myrrh.

Then we get to the tragic side of Christmas, the part that doesn't get told very often.

While Mary and Joseph were wondering about the shepherds and the astrologers, Joseph was warned in a dream to get out of

Bethlehem. Which he did. So the young family had to escape to Egypt and live there as refugees. And sure enough, the king decided to eliminate the possibility of any future contender for the throne and slaughtered all the baby boys in Bethlehem. There is a deeply tragic side to the beauty of the Christmas story.

A Crowded Stable

The story of Jesus' birth is one we tell over and over every Christmas. We sing carols about the kings and the shepherds, and in recent years, we've added the littlest angel and the little drummer boy and a batch of others till that stable is getting pretty crowded.

The stories are sometimes beautiful and often fun, but sometimes they get us away from the basic point. Jesus, the most important human being ever to walk the earth, the "son of God," was born in a smelly, unsanitary barn among the cows and chickens and cockroaches, and his parents were pretty ordinary folks.

There's a kind of cosmic humor here. The child of God—"King of King and Lord of Lords" to use more traditional language—is born into the worst imaginable circumstances.

Who Says It's Logical?

What's the point of the story?

The point is that in a deep and mysterious way, Jesus was both a human being and also God. Not half God and half human, but completely human and completely God, and if that confuses you, you're in good company.

We call it a paradox. Logically, it doesn't hang together, but who said the Christian faith is logical? It makes sense to Christians because we experience Jesus both as God and as a human.

The whole Christmas story is one of contrasts. The child is special but very ordinary. Jesus is born in a barn, but there's a special star over the stable. The stink of manure is mingled with the fragrance of frankincense brought by wealthy astrologers who kneel in the dirt before a simple child. The baby is honored with extravagant titles, but his parents have to pick up and run because a dictator wants to slaughter their child. The Child of God is a refugee.

The Bible stories are told, not so much to record history, but to help the teller and the hearer of the story understand in a way that goes beyond logical argument, who this Jesus was, and what he was about. That holds true for the stories of his birth, as it does for the rest of the stories about Jesus.

God, Give Us a Break!

The Christmas story is the *hors d'oeuvre*. Far too many people stop there and miss the *entrée*. The main part of the Jesus story begins about 30 years after the accounts of his birth.

Jesus begins his work by being baptized by his cousin John, in the Jordan River. After that, Jesus goes into the desert where he spends a long time wrestling with questions about what he is going to do and how he is going to do it.

Jesus knew that the Messiah idea had been around for several hundred years. The people of Israel were expecting a Messiah, someone who would come and liberate them from the military dictatorship under which they lived. Life wasn't easy in that part of the world. Politically, economically, religiously, things were a mess. Not much different than now.

The Romans occupied the country, which meant the Hebrews had to pay heavy taxes to a foreign government. Even their own leaders were sometimes corrupt. The constant prayer of the Jewish people was, in effect, "God, give us a break. Send us someone to get us out of this mess!"

They wanted a Messiah, which means "the anointed one" or "chosen one." The Greek translation was *Christos* or in English, Christ. This Christ would get them out of their jam. This Messiah, they figured, would round up an army and kick the Romans out on their backsides. Or, as some might say today, "Nuke 'em."

Jesus knew perfectly well what the people wanted, which is why he went out there into the desert to get his head straight. It is always very tempting to give people what they want, instead of what they need.

It was hell out there in the desert: a soul-searching, soul-searing hell. But Jesus came out of that desert experience after 40 long days and nights determined to do what God wanted him to do. Jesus knew that wouldn't win him any popularity contests.

God Has Chosen Me . . .

Jesus headed straight for the synagogue, the Jewish "church" in his hometown. The folks in the village thought it was nice to have the young man home again, and they asked Jesus to read the scripture. He chose a passage from an ancient writer known as Isaiah. It goes like this:

The Spirit of the Lord is upon me, because God has chosen me to bring good news to the poor. God has sent me to proclaim liberty to the captives and recovery of sight to the blind, to set free the oppressed, and announce that the time has come for the Lord's people to be saved.

Some Christians call this passage from Isaiah Jesus' job description. It's a poem that's full of metaphors, with many layers of meaning. I'm tempted to spend ten pages talking about what it implies. Or maybe a whole book or two. I'll try to resist.

Don't get hung up on the specifics of that passage for now. The reason I quoted it here is because I want you to notice what it *doesn't* say. It says nothing about Jesus proclaiming himself Lord High Everything. It says nothing about honor and glory and power for Jesus, even though some other writers in the Bible tried to lay that on him.

What it *does* say is that Jesus had come to do things for the "poor," the "captives," the "blind," and the "oppressed." That theme occurs again and again in the stories of his life. Jesus set out to help others. He took the side of the people who needed it most—the underdogs in his society.

Don't Overdo the Miracles

It's important to remember that little fact, because when people first start reading or hearing the story of Jesus, they are very impressed by the miracles he performed. Being impressed by the miracles is not a bad place to start.

But if that's where you end up, if the main thing you have in your head about Jesus is his miracles, you miss the point. Jesus did miracles because he loved people. He wanted to help them. The love Jesus demonstrated is far more important than details of the miracles themselves.

That's the main difference between Jesus and a wide variety of magicians and faith healers who went around entertaining the crowds in those days, just as they do now. Jesus didn't do miracles for their publicity value. In fact he usually told people to keep quiet about the miracles. Jesus was not much interested in being popular.

Jesus didn't go around saying, "Hey look, folks. I'm God! Believe everything I say." In fact, Jesus never once referred to himself as God.

People only began to think of Jesus as God in human flesh in the years *after* his death. It was only when they looked back on the life of Jesus, when they reflected on who he was and what he did, that the first Christians understood the dynamic, powerful gift they had been given.

Here's a suggestion about the miracles. If this is new territory for you, don't make up your mind about the pieces of this jigsaw puzzle until you've had a look at the complete picture. Like many other aspects of Christianity, it's hard to see the significance of one part, unless you have a more complete picture in your head.

Parables

The basic thing about Jesus was that he went around loving people, and showing that love in different ways. Jesus went to great lengths to explain and to show how much God loved everyone.

Jesus used a literary device called the parable, a short story made up to illustrate a point. Even though you may not have read anything in the Bible, you've probably heard some of his parables. They're world famous.

For instance, you may have heard the story of the Good Samaritan. It was a parable Jesus told after a lawyer came up and wanted to know what had to be done to find "eternal life."

"What did they teach you in law school?" was the essence of what Jesus asked the lawyer. Of course, in those days, all law was religious law. The idea that religion was somehow separate from the rest of life didn't occur to the lawyer or to Jesus.

The lawyer gave the answer he'd learned in school. "Love the Lord your God with all your heart, with all your soul, and with all your mind, and your neighbor as yourself."

"So? Go do it," said Jesus.

But the lawyer wanted to quibble. "Who is my neighbor?"

That's when Jesus told the story of the Good Samaritan. It helps, when you hear this story, to know that Samaritans and Jews didn't get along too well. From the Hebrew point of view, Samaritans were trash. Jesus, a Jew himself, was telling the story to a group of Jews.

The story goes basically like this. This fellow, a Jew, was going down the road from Jerusalem to Jericho, and a bunch of thugs grabbed him, beat him to a pulp, took his money, and left him half-dead on the side of the road.

Down the road comes a Jewish priest who takes one look at the traveler all bloody and broken on the side of the road, and hightails it out of there. A few minutes later, along comes another leading citizen of the town, who turns out to be in even more of a hurry than the priest.

Finally, along comes a Samaritan. Guess who picks the fellow up, takes him to an inn, and patches him up? The despised Samaritan. Not only that but the Samaritan leaves some money with the innkeeper and says, "Take care of this poor guy. If it costs any more, I'll be back in a few days and I'll pay you."

Then Jesus throws the question back at the lawyer. "Who do you suppose was the neighbor to the man who got beaten up by the thugs?"

The answer was obvious. "The Samaritan who picked the man up and helped him."

"So? Go do it!" Jesus repeated.

Two Brothers and Their Dad

Jesus didn't make many long speeches or sermons. Mostly he told stories—parables. Aside from everything else, these parables are remarkable examples of fine literature. Even if you don't believe what Christians say about him, you have to admit Jesus was a first-class storyteller.

The story of the Prodigal Son is a classic. In telling the story, Jesus was trying to give us a glimpse of what God was like. The "Father" in this story is God.

He was a wealthy farmer, a highly respected person in the community. And this father had two sons.

The youngest son was not a model child. In fact, he shocked the whole town by going up to his dad and saying, "Hey, Pops! When you die, I get my slice of the family fortune. Why do I have to wait that long? Give it to me now."

If it had been me, I would have wanted to whup this punk's backside and send him out to weed the turnips. But the father in the parable said, "Yes," which everybody in the whole town, especially the elder brother, agreed was a bad, bad, move. The boy would just waste the money.

They were right, of course. The kid left home with all that cash in his pocket. For a while, he had a marvelous time: eating, spending, drinking, living it up. The fun lasted as long as the money.

One morning, he woke up with a hangover and a major cash-flow problem. Finally, the kid got so desperate and so hungry, he got a job on a pig farm.

A pig farm! This kid is Jewish, remember? For Jewish people, pork is vile.

Soon the younger son gets to thinking that the pigs are eating better than he is. He wonders if maybe the old man might be soft-hearted enough to give him a job on the farm. As a hired hand. Certainly not as a son. At least he'd be able to eat.

So the kid up and heads for home, realizing that he's blown it, more and more wanting to turn his own life around, memorizing a little speech he's going to make to the old man.

Frankly, the kid doesn't give it much of a chance. He's disgraced his father. His dad is now the laughing stock of the countryside. The kid wouldn't get the time of day from a typical father. But what has he got to lose?

The kid's father isn't typical. When the kid is still quite a ways from home, his father hears about it, forgets his dignity and goes running out to meet him.

Running!

The father doesn't even have the dignity to make the son grovel a bit. Not only that, the old man is just busting with so much happiness, that he throws a huge party for the kid.

Meanwhile, big brother is out behind the barn having a royal snit. His dad comes and begs him to come join the party.

"No way!" says big brother. "Look, I've worked for years here on the farm. Have you ever thrown a party for me? But this kid of yours goes off and blows your money on a bunch of hookers. And you throw a banquet, for Pete's sake!"

"Son, listen!" says the old man. "I've always loved you. And you've always known that. But your brother was dead and is alive again. He was lost but now he's found. Now that's something to celebrate."

Favoring the Underdog

In those days, as today, that kind of story goes directly against the way in which most of us think. "Spare the rod and spoil the child," is the way many parents would have said it. "Tough love," is what some authorities advocate. "He got himself into that mess." "He made his bed. Let him lie in it!"

Jesus seemed to be saying that God doesn't react the way we do. God's love is free. Like the kid who blew it all, you don't have to deserve God's love to get it. All you have to do is want it. Even if you've messed up your own life completely, even if it's totally your fault, even if you don't deserve any consideration,

God is just aching to love you and to help you turn your life around.

The establishment people in Jesus' day didn't like that kind of God one bit.

"We deserve what we've got because we are better people," they told themselves. "God loves us more than all that no good riffraff. Don't tell me God loves the drunken wino or the wired hooker as much as God loves me!"

There was the incident with Zacchaeus. Zacc was a tax collector who worked for the Romans. The Roman soldiers ran the country with an iron hand. To make things worse, Zacc had a habit of skimming a bit extra off the top for himself. He wasn't likely to win the Citizen of the Year award.

Jesus was on his way into town and, as often happened, quite a crowd had gathered, curious about this preacher who seemed to be getting so much attention. Zacc was curious too, but he was also one of the shortest guys in town. Standing in the crowd, all he could see was other people's backsides.

Zacc climbed a tree to get a better look. That's where Jesus spotted him.

"Zacchaeus," said Jesus. "Come down out of that tree. How about inviting me over to your house for dinner?"

You could hear the crowd sucking air through their teeth. What kind of a religious leader is this that invites himself into the house of a rotten traitor like Zacc, the collaborator with the enemy, the cheat?

The Bible doesn't tell us what Jesus and Zacchaeus talked about over dinner. But it does tell us that at the end of it, Zacc was a different person. He went to all the people he had cheated and paid them back four times what he'd cheated them out of. And then Zacchaeus gave half of everything he had to charity.

Nevertheless, the people who saw all this still didn't like it. "A religious leader should stay away from scum like that!" they said.

Jesus was acting out a parable that made an important point. The people were right. Zacchaeus was not exactly a model citizen. But he was one of God's children, no matter what he had done. And so Jesus reached out his hand in love to this sick and lonely man.

Jesus was rocking the boat. "It's all very noble," said the people, "but you just don't do that sort of thing."

The leaders in the community found Jesus' behavior particularly threatening. Soon they were figuring out ways to get him. Several times they set up a situation in which they hoped to trap Jesus, to get him to say something incriminating.

It Takes Two to Tango

For instance, in those days the penalty for adultery was death by stoning. The law stated quite clearly that the penalty was for both men and women, but it never seemed to get applied to men. Only women got caught committing adultery, even though they knew perfectly well it takes two to tango.

The establishment leaders hauled a woman up to Jesus, and threw her down on the ground.

"She was caught in the very act of adultery. The law says she should be executed by stoning," they said.

These men (yes, they were all men) knew that Jesus always went to the side of the person who was getting the worst of the deal. "A bleeding heart," they probably called him. They expected Jesus would try and get the woman off, and then they could accuse him of counseling someone to break the law.

Jesus didn't bite. He bent over and wrote something on the ground, though the Bible doesn't tell us what it was. Maybe it was something about the man whom she was caught with, but who wasn't hauled up for stoning.

At any rate, he looked the woman's accusers in the eye and said, "Let the one who is without sin throw the first stone."

You could have cut the silence with a knife. One by one they drifted off, until finally there was just Jesus, and the woman sobbing on the ground.

Quietly Jesus asked her, "Where is everybody? Is there no one left to condemn you?"

"No one, sir," she said.

"Then I don't condemn you either. Go, but don't sin any more."

Jesus and Women

Jesus obviously didn't like adultery, but he liked even less the kind of treatment the woman was getting. In fact, Jesus' attitude toward women was radical, in the context of his day.

In that time and culture (and sometimes even today in our modern "enlightened" society), women were regarded simply as the property of a man. In Jesus' day, a woman first belonged to her father, then later to her husband. In lists of a man's possessions, women would be listed along with the cattle, with about as many rights.

It was even considered wrong for a man to have a conversation with a woman, especially in public. And it was against the law to talk to women about religion. A woman's function, aside from the work she could do, was to please men and bear children.

That's why it was so radical when Jesus carried on long conversations with women, sometimes foreign women—which was even more revolutionary. Jesus talked with them about deep, religious subjects. Jesus numbered women among his disciples and friends. It was, as they said, "most unusual."

Jesus seemed to have a talent for rubbing the authorities the wrong way. Once, the authorities confronted him with the fact that his disciples were breaking the law by picking corn on the Sabbath, the Jewish holy day. But Jesus said to them, "The Sabbath was made for people. People were not made for the Sabbath."

In other words, the law and teaching of religion were intended to help people live fully and well. Not the other way around.

Was Jesus Religious?

None of this won Jesus much popularity with the authorities, but ordinary folk were beginning to crowd around him. He talked in a way they could understand. He made sense.

Jesus must have been a friendly and a happy person. He seemed to get invited to quite a few parties. There are several accounts of the children hanging around. Kids don't hang around a sourpuss.

Looking back on the story of Jesus, if you don't read it too carefully, it's very easy to get a picture of a person who was hardly human at all, someone who walked around with an angelic look on his face, who never lost his cool, never put his foot in his mouth, never got fed up, angry, tired.

In fact, many religious artists have painted just that kind of picture of Jesus. They've tried so hard to make him look so "holy," that mostly they make him look half-stoned.

Frankly, I don't think Jesus looked or acted very "religious." He seemed to enjoy being with very earthy people, folk in the markets and on the street. He was even accused of being a friend of hookers and drunks.

Christians have been struggling with the question of who Jesus was for 2,000 years. It's hard to think of Jesus as completely human and completely God at the same time. Often we concentrate on Jesus as God, and forget that Jesus was also human, that he cried, that he got angry, that he was not Superman in sandals.

Scared Stiff

Let's get back to the story.

Jesus went around teaching and healing and talking with people for about three years before the roof fell in. Jesus seemed to know that if he kept needling the authorities, they'd eventually get back at him. His disciples tried to convince Jesus to take a long holiday in the hills, to stay out of Jerusalem till things cooled down a bit. Jesus was tempted. He was human, and afraid. Very afraid.

He must have been afraid. Scared stiff. Otherwise, his horrible death would be nothing more than a publicity gimmick staged by a Hollywood stunt actor who knew there was no real danger involved.

Even in the middle of his fear, Jesus was convinced that God was calling on him to see it through. Still, it must have been just as hard for Jesus as for anyone else who is facing death.

The Upper Room

Knowing things were coming to a head, Jesus arranged to have a very important meal with the twelve followers or disciples who had hung in with him for the last three years or so. This was to be the Passover meal.

That meal with the disciples was one of the key events of Jesus' life. But to understand why we feel that meal was so important, we've got to go on a little side trip to explain the Passover and its significance.

Jewish people had observed the Passover for thousands of years, and still do. The Passover is usually celebrated by families to help them remember an event that goes way back into the mists of history, to a time when the Hebrew (Jewish) people were living in Egypt as slaves. The Egyptian pharaohs (kings) used them like biodegradable bulldozers that could be worked to death and then simply discarded.

The Bible tells the story of how a man named Moses was chosen to be God's agent to lead these Hebrews out of Egypt. That wasn't as easy as it sounds. It took more than a call to a friendly travel agent. It took courage, suffering, and terrible loss.

Jews, Christians, and Muslims all believe that Moses, with God's help, led the Hebrew people out of slavery and into the promised land of Israel. In that struggle to be free, the Hebrew people relearned the ancient and very special relationship God had with them. They spent 40 years wandering around in a trackless desert, where they learned what it meant to be a chosen people—chosen to act on God's behalf.

The Hebrews were chosen to be a "people of the covenant." And that word "covenant" is very important to both Jews and Christians. A covenant is an agreement. It can be a legal contract, or simply an understanding between two people.

But for Christians and Jews it means something more. I like to think of the covenant as a kind of family relationship. My children will always be my children, regardless of how well or how badly we may treat each other. And I will always be "Dad," even when I become weak and senile. This is a family covenant—a special relationship.

In the Hebrew part of the Bible this covenant is put into starkly simple words: "I will be your God and you shall be my people."

The Hebrews didn't always do a great job of being the "covenant people." Sometimes they acted as if they'd never heard of God—as if they had no idea what it meant to be a "chosen" people. But the covenant was there, whether they lived up to it or not.

The story of God leading the Hebrews out of Egypt, of God shaping them in the desert to become a covenant people, is dramatic and beautiful. It is one of the central stories in the Jewish, Muslim, and Christian faiths. For people in the Jewish faith, it is the central story.

And part of the story is about God's attempt to convince Pharaoh to let the Hebrew people out of Egypt. God sent an angel of death, which hit the homes of the Egyptians, but passed over the Hebrews. So Jewish people celebrate that "passing over" every year in the Passover feast.

It was this celebration that brought Jesus and his disciples together for their last meal before Jesus' death. And in its turn, that event has become central to the Christian story.

An Object Lesson

On the surface that meal seems very simple and ordinary. Jesus and the disciples rented a room, and the twelve of them gathered together for what we now call "the Last Supper."

Jesus began the Passover celebration by giving his disciples a little object lesson. He washed their feet. It was considered a courtesy, when someone came into your home, to have one of the servants wash your guest's feet.

Washing feet was not considered a very dignified job. The disciples raised a ruckus when Jesus started doing it. Jesus was, after all, their leader, and it wasn't right for him to be doing a slave's work. One of them, Peter, protested that if anyone was going to wash feet, he should be washing Jesus' feet.

"Try to understand," said Jesus. "The most important one among you must be like the least important, and the leader must be like the servant."

Again, Jesus was swimming upstream, making the point that a leader, especially a religious leader, must be a servant to those led. He was also showing the disciples who he was. Jesus saw himself as a servant. A slave.

After that acted parable, Jesus and the disciples sat down to eat. They ate a simple, ordinary meal together. The memory of that meal has evolved into the central ritual in almost every Christian church. Some call it the Eucharist, others Holy Communion or the Lord's Supper.

During the meal, Jesus took a piece of bread and said a prayer of thanks. Then he broke the bread and passed it around to his disciples saying, "This bread, my body, broken for you. Do this in memory of me."

Then Jesus took a goblet of wine and said, "This cup is God's new covenant sealed with my blood, which is poured out for you."

A "new covenant," a new understanding of that old and very special relationship with God. A new covenant that is lived out, not through special privileges or protection, but through a special understanding that helps us, if we're willing, to live out the love of God in a hurting and hurtful world.

So the supper Jesus had with his disciples in that upper room took God's gift of a covenant going back thousands of years, and offered it to us as a gift to the future.

Earlier, I mentioned that Christians read the Bible through a particular set of lenses, with a particular understanding nourished by 2,000 years of trying to live out the Christian faith. Nowhere does this apply more than it does to the stories of the Last Supper.

We read the story of that event, knowing it was the last meal Jesus ate with his disciples. We read it with the terrible-wonderful story of Jesus' death in mind. And his new life with us.

More important, we read that story knowing that when we gather as a Christian community to remember that meal in what we call the Eucharist or Lord's Supper or Communion, something deep and fundamental happens. In a way that goes beyond our understanding, we share in Jesus' life, death, and resurrection.

It's an impossible thing to explain. It's a beautiful thing to experience.

No Other Way

The story of what happened to Jesus in the day or two after that supper reads like a bad dream. The authorities finally decided they simply had to be rid of this troublemaker, and paid Judas, one of Jesus' friends, to turn him in.

Even at that point, Jesus could have made his getaway. Quite easily. In fact, that's what Jesus wanted, and that's what his disciples wanted. So he got down on his knees and prayed and prayed. "God, if it's possible, don't make me go through with this! Please!" But

Jesus wanted something even more than to escape the pain, and that was to be faithful to the will of God.

There was no other way. There still isn't. Greed, corruption, selfishness, the lust for power, hate, prejudice, fear always result in suffering and death, often suffering and death for the innocent.

Jesus' death was God's huge cosmic object lesson to us. And most of the world still hasn't learned it, which is why we often speak of Jesus as still being crucified, every day, by our greed, corruption, selfishness, lust for power, hate, prejudice and fear.

The charge they had laid against Jesus was treason, a political crime. For that the penalty was death on a cross, one of the most cruel, hideous, painful forms of execution ever invented. Jesus died like a common crook.

A Footnote to History

That should have been the end of the story. Jesus was dead. He was buried. It was messy, but at least it was over.

The story of Jesus should have been a very small footnote to history. "Local preacher gets carried away and the authorities stomp on him." No big deal.

Except that one of Jesus' followers, Mary of Magdala, went with two other disciples to the tomb. And this is where we came in near the beginning of the chapter.

Mary and the others were going to anoint Jesus' body with spices, a gesture of respect and love similar in some ways to our custom of putting flowers on a grave. When they got to the tomb, they discovered Jesus' body was missing. Grave robbers, they figured.

But Mary stayed behind to have a good cry, and through her tears she saw a person she thought at first was the man who took care of the grounds. Then she recognized him. It was Jesus! And he told her to go tell the rest of the disciples.

Which she did. Running and yelling and whooping. And of course the other disciples didn't believe her. Not at first anyway.

Then Jesus appeared to the disciples several times, walking with them, talking with them, teaching them, and telling them to go out and spread the Word. That's "Word" with a capital "W."

And the Word! Not a collection of words in any book. Not even the Bible. But the Word as lived by Jesus who was the Christ.

And the meaning of that Word? That life is stronger than death. That hope is greater than despair. That love is more powerful than hate. That in spite of the worst we humans can do, God conquers sin and corruption and death.

The Word: the birth, the life, the teaching, the death, the resurrection of Jesus gives us a clear and true idea of who God is, of what God is, how God wants us to live, and who God wants us to be!

No, it does not mean that God did a quick CPR on Jesus, who was only clinically dead. Jesus was completely dead all right. But God brought Jesus, the Christ, the Messiah, into a new kind of life, a resurrected life, a life that's promised to all of us!

The Jesus Experience

Now you'll understand why I couldn't give a handy-dandy definition of God in the first chapter. For a Christian there is no such definition. The only way we know God is by experiencing Jesus. You can't put a person into a formula or a slogan, even though people have often tried to do that.

That's why all those metaphors for God in the second chapter were useful, but unsatisfying. None of them really rang completely true. It's when we experience the power of Christ that we can say, "Aha! Now we know what God is like!"

Or as one little girl apparently told her mother, "Jesus is God with skin on."

That's why I kept insisting that we have to get a handle on who Jesus was and what he was about, before we can really approach the Bible or the rest of Christian history. Because that's the set of lenses through which we see the rest of the long, long story.

The actual story of Jesus only takes up less than one tenth of the Bible. Before it, comes the whole Old Testament, a marvelous collection of material that leads up to the story of Jesus—in Christian eyes anyway. And the Jesus story is followed by the account of what the first Christians did and thought and worried about following Jesus' resurrection.

The Christian story doesn't end with the last word in the Bible either. There's the long, colorful story about what happened to the Christian church between the last accounts in the Bible and today.

It's a marvelous, creative, sometimes funny, sometimes depressing, sometimes seamy story of people struggling in many different ways to be faithful to God's call, of people falling flat on their faces, but getting up and trying one more time.

Christians see their history, which includes the Bible, as the magnificent saga of a God who is active in human history.

Others see the Christian story as a colorful collection of obscure myths, doubtful legends, questionable history and quite a few lies.

Either way, it is a marvelous story.

—4—

The Bible

Humble confession time.

I've been sitting here trying to figure out how to start a chapter on the Bible. And I'm having trouble because Christians have spent so much energy fussing over this book, arguing about what it is, how it should be used, and what authority it has. Some of that bickering has been downright unchristian.

I was trying to think of something to start with that everyone would agree on. I didn't come up with much, except that we all agree it's important. Very important. Maybe that's why we spend so much time squabbling over it.

I promised not to try to talk you into one particular point of view but it's hard to avoid taking a viewpoint in a chapter on the Bible. Everybody has an opinion on this book and I'm no exception. So let's plunge in and do the best we can. But it does emphasize the importance of reading other books besides this one on the subject.

The word "bible" simply means "book." Actually, the Bible is a bunch of books, all collected into one volume.

The many books of the Bible are not always in chronological order. In most cases we don't know for sure when they were written. They are loosely arranged according to the kind of writing they contain, and within that, in approximate chronological order. But the arrangement is more traditional than logical.

The first part of the Bible is usually called the "Old Testament," which means "old covenant." If you are Jewish, that's your whole Bible. In fact, many people now call it the Hebrew scripture, which is probably more correct than Old Testament.

If you are Muslim, the Hebrew scripture is a prelude to the Koran. If you are a Christian, you have the Hebrew scripture and the Christian scripture together in the Bible. The Christian scripture is usually called the "New Testament" which begins with the birth of

Jesus and takes us through the early years of the Christian church.

Things Have Changed

The Hebrew scripture was originally written in Hebrew, and the Christian scripture in Greek. For many years, the only accepted English translation was known as the King James Version. It dates from 1611, near the time of Shakespeare. If you have an old family Bible somewhere, or one you were given as a child, it's probably a King James (or Authorized) version of the Bible.

In its time, the King James Version was a remarkable work, reflecting fine scholarship and a fantastic command of the English language. But with advances in archaeology and linguistics, we now have much more accurate translations than people did in 1611.

Even more important, though, our English language has changed. Many English words simply mean different things to us now than they did to people in 1611. For instance, when they did the King James Version, the translators deliberately used "thou" when addressing God, because in those days, "thou" was the common form used for addressing an equal. The idea was to make God more accessible, less distant. They didn't want to use "you" because that was reserved for the upper crust, as in "Your Royal Highness."

Now our English usage of "thou" and "you" has flip-flopped, and people complain when new translations address God as "you" rather than "thou." It makes God sound too common.

If you want a very simple, easy-to-read translation, I'd suggest the *Good News Bible*. Because it is written using limited vocabulary, some compromises have been made on accuracy. That's why most people prefer the New Revised Standard Version (NRSV). It was done by some of the world's best translators so it is easily the most accurate. They were careful to avoid the sexist language that was not in the original Greek or Hebrew but was put in by the translators in many other versions. And—what appeals to me most of all—they've kept much of the beautiful language and ca-

dence of the King James Version. Most clergy
I know use the NRSV.

Other good translations are *The New English Bible*, *The Jerusalem Bible*, and *The New International Version*. I'd suggest you stay clear of *The Way*, which is simple and clear but very misleading in places. In fact, it's not a translation at all, but a paraphrase.

Don't try at first to read the King James (or Authorized) translation. The language is too much like Shakespeare: beautiful, but often confusing. And the King James Version is sometimes inaccurate too.

Almost all bookstores have various translations of the Bible available, but the widest variety are in the religious bookstores. If you want to get serious about Bible study, get the *Oxford Annotated New Revised Standard Version* which has very helpful footnotes and cross-references.

History, Literature, or Rules?

In any translation, and any way you look at it, the Bible is an amazing book. And it is constantly one of the world's best-sellers.

For starters, it is a remarkably accurate record. Archaeologists have often been amazed at how well the Bible has recorded historical events.

But the Bible is not primarily a history book. The Bible is remarkable literature. Any course on the history of writing in Western culture has to spend a major hunk of time on the Bible. There's magnificent poetry, high drama, adventurous sagas, pithy epigrams, corny melodrama and even a bit of eroticism. It soars to the heights of literary greatness, and occasionally gets as down and dirty as the steamiest TV drama you can name.

The Bible has influenced the writing and the language of European and Middle Eastern culture. Our English language is full of phrases and epigrams from the Bible. In books of commonly used quotations, as in literature courses, the Bible always tops the list. Personally, I often open the Bible just because it's such a "good read." Many people don't realize this because they've been put off by the archaic language of the King James translation.

But the Bible is not primarily a book of literature.

There is great wisdom, and many useful rules, in the Bible. In its pages, you can find instruction on everything from how to dress, to how to clean your body, to advice about marriage, children, politics, money, and death.

Some of the wise sayings and a few of the rules contradict each other. Down through the centuries, people have read the Bible to find the specifics of how they should order their lives. With mixed results.

But the Bible is not primarily a handy guide to daily living, and *it most certainly is not a rule book*.

Christians Don't Believe in the Bible

Christians believe that God is involved in their lives. The Bible is a record of how, over the course of several thousand years, God was involved in the life of the Hebrews (Old Testament) and the Christians (New Testament).

So when we read the Bible, we appreciate the history and the literature and the good advice for living. But it's all secondary. What we're looking for is something we call "revelation"—the way in which God has been revealed to people.

Let's get one thing straight. Neither Christians nor Jews "believe in the Bible." We believe in *God*. God doesn't point to the Bible. The Bible points to God.

Christians believe in God as revealed to us through Jesus. We learn about Jesus and about God's actions from the Bible. The Bible is the most important way we can know about God. Not the only way, but easily the most important way.

Down through the centuries, Hebrew scholars, and in their turn the Christian leaders, looked at many ancient writings and selected the ones which would eventually be called "scripture." They looked for those writings which seemed most clearly to show how God was active in the lives of the covenant community and through the events of history.

Those venerable church leaders didn't always agree, and they still don't. For instance, there are differences in the Catholic and Protestant Bibles. Martin Luther, one of the early leaders in the Protestant movement, was a major figure in deciding what went into the Protestant collection of writings. Luther didn't want the book of James to be included in the Bible. He called it "an epistle of straw," but he lost the argument. The book is there.

Is the Bible True?

Much energy has been wasted by Christians arguing about whether the Bible is "true." Some argue that the scribes who wrote down the words of the Bible were like secretaries taking down dictation. Every word is spoken by God.

At the other extreme are those who insist the Bible is "inspired" but only in the same way that Shakespeare or Annie Dillard or any other good writer may be inspired. Most Christians are somewhere between those two extremes.

When you look at the history of how we got our Bible, you realize that the argument about whether or not "the Bible is true" is rather silly. It's a pretty recent argument, in the sense that it's only been bothering people for a couple of hundred years. That question didn't occur to the people who brought the ancient writing together into what we now call the Bible.

Those people had good, healthy arguments about the value and truth of various parts of the ancient religious writings. But to respond to a question like "Is the Bible true?" you first have to figure out what you mean by a word like "true."

There are people who claim that unless every word in the Bible is "true" nothing in the Bible can be believed. "How do you know every word in the Bible is true?" "Because the Bible says so!" (It doesn't really!) It's a circular argument that wouldn't stand up in a kangaroo court.

The claim that every word of the Bible is literally true is not traditional Christian teaching. Claims about the "infallibility" or "inerrancy" of the Bible have really come about as an overreaction to scientific critics who asked some tough (and legitimate) questions. When people feel cornered, they yell a lot and dig in their heels. You can see that with a number of Christian denominations and sects. But that kind of reaction is not true of most Christians.

Most of us believe that we can hear the voice of God when we read the Bible. That doesn't mean that God's "words" are the same words as are in the Bible. The Bible is traditionally known as "a means of revelation." As we study the Bible, wrestle with its meaning, and apply it to our lives, we hear the voice of God, though not always in specific words.

We can only understand these things by relating them to experiences in our own lives. This book is dedicated to Jim Taylor, a friend and colleague of many years. When he read a draft of this book, he wrote a critique that was tough and pointed. Some of the things he said made me uncomfortable.

But even though Jim didn't say it, throughout his critique, I felt his deep friendship. I knew Jim cared about me and about this writing project.

In a similar but much more profound way, we sense God speaking to us through the words of the Bible.

Revelation, God being revealed to humans, has never been limited to the Bible. When the last book of the Bible was written down about a hundred or so years after the death of Jesus, God didn't stop communicating with people.

Christians have always believed that God is ready to communicate with anyone who is willing to listen. And people in all times and cultures and places have been listening. That listening has changed their lives. As they lived out their understanding of what they heard God communicating, they learned even more about "the will of God."

Every time we go back to the Bible—and as Christians we do that constantly—our understanding of what God is trying to say to us through the Bible is made richer by the other ways in which we have been experiencing God in our lives. And the way other people have been experiencing God enriches our understanding as well.

Proof-texting

The Bible points us to God, who communicates with us when we read the Bible carefully and with an open mind.

Unfortunately, some of the ways in which people use the Bible can block God's communication. One of those is called "proof-texting."

Proof-texting takes phrases or segments from the Bible, one from here, another from there, and uses them to "prove" a preselected point of view. The process leads to all kinds of crazy conclusions, because you can find enough snippets of this and that to support anything you wish.

For instance, in one part of the Bible (Isaiah 2:4, if you want to look it up) it says, "They will beat their swords into plowshares and their spears into pruning hooks."

But in another place (Joel 3:10) it says exactly the opposite. "Beat your plowshares into swords and your pruning hooks into spears." Both doves and hawks quote the Bible to back up their arguments.

Proof-texting has been used very effectively to support slavery, racial segregation, polygamy, incest, war, murder, and even drunkenness. It is often used to support sexism. As somebody once said, "a proof-text out of context becomes a pretext."

Proof-texting is an abuse of the Bible, even when done by very good Christians, and even if we happen to agree with the conclusions that are reached.

There's the story of one misguided fellow who believed he could open his Bible at any point and whatever phrase caught his eye, that was God's word for him for that moment. So he opened the Bible and read, "Judas went and hanged himself." He swallowed hard and opened the Bible in another spot. It said, "Go thou and do likewise."

Studying the Bible

Learning the Bible can be a very rewarding and helpful experience. But people who pick a dusty old Bible off the shelf and start reading on page one often find they don't get very far. So here are a few suggestions if you want to get into the Bible.

First, get one of the newer translations.

Second, if you have any connections with a church or other religious community, get involved in a Bible study group. The best Bible study happens when you work with others, especially if there's some good trained leadership.

Third, check the reading list at the back of this book. It's especially important to have a general understanding of the life and teachings of Jesus because they are the core of the Bible for Christians. In the Christian church, everything else in the Bible is judged in the light of who Jesus was and what he taught.

Another thing to note about the Bible. Some parts are more important and useful than others. Along with God's revelation that has shaped the world, you'll find delightful bits of folklore, history, ancient medical advice and other fascinating stuff. Especially in the Hebrew scriptures. That's not a put-down, but let's face it, instructions on how to bake bread are hardly in the same league with the Ten Commandments.

As you read the Bible, please remember that every part of the Bible must be read in the context of the whole sweeping story of God's work amidst the human race. The Bible is the primary window through which we can see God. But it is certainly not the only window. God has been active, and God is still active, in the lives and the work of people around the world.

So by all means study the Bible, but recognize that it's not the sort of job you knock off quickly between football games on TV. What you get out of your Bible will depend pretty much on how much mental sweat you put into your study of it.

The Bible Is Addressed to the Church

A few paragraphs back, I suggested that it's best to study the Bible in a group at a church. My reason for suggesting that, as opposed to studying the Bible on your own, is related to a concept that is basic to the Christian faith. I mentioned that the two parts of the Bible are generally called the Old and the New Testament, and testament means covenant.

God's covenant is not with individuals, but with a people. Christians believe that God's first covenant was with the Hebrew people. The renewal of that covenant, which Jesus spoke about with his disciples, was with the Christian church.

As you get into the Bible, you'll realize that when God speaks through the Old Testament prophets, God is speaking to the Hebrew nation. And if you read the opening paragraphs of the books in the New Testament, you find most of them addressed to the whole church.

Individuals studying the Bible and drawing their own conclusions can come up with some marvelous insights and some pretty kooky ideas. Individual Bible study has led to everything from the great reformations to the Jonestown massacre.

I think that's why the Bible is addressed to the community rather than to individuals. It's a way each of us can check our insight or inspiration against what Christians have known down through the centuries and around the world. Studying the Bible in the church community should not stifle us as individuals. It's simply a recognition that "none of us is as smart as all of us."

The Old Covenant

Now that we've walked around the Bible a bit, let's open it and take a quick look inside.

Unfortunately, our peek into the Bible will be a little like sticking your nose in the door of a bakery. You'll get a great whiff of the delicious assortment of bagels and muffins inside, but you won't have time to even pop in and buy a doughnut. Sorry about that! But the bakery is open 24 hours a day, seven days a week, and you can come back anytime. I hope you will, and sample everything from the cream puffs to the black bread.

At the beginning of the Bible you'll find the Pentateuch, which literally means "five tools" and refers to the first five books of the Bible. Pentateuch is a good word to remember if you like using heavy-duty words to impress people.

The Pentateuch is the oldest part of the Bible. To the Jewish people it is the very heart of holy scripture. The first two books, Genesis (beginnings) and Exodus (moving out) contain the basic stories—the deepest convictions of the Judeo-Christian tradition.

Adam and Eve and All That

The very first part of the first book of Genesis tells two stories about creation. Yes, two.

The first one is about God's creation of the world in six days. God pronounced the world "very good" and then rested. The second account is the well-known story of Adam and Eve and the garden and the snake.

These are not stories of *how* God created the world. They are neither scientific nor historic. The first story tries to answer the question of *why* God created, and what that creation *means*. The second one deals with questions such as how come there is so much sin, and why don't people pay more attention to what God is saying, and why do we have to work so hard, and why does it hurt to have babies?

If we try to read these biblical accounts as scientific papers or historical documents, we get hung up in silly arguments that have nothing to do with the profound religious statements that are being made in those stories. Read them for their powerful symbols, their stirring images, the striking metaphors, and you'll discover marvelous depths of meaning.

Ten Commandments

Also in the Pentateuch we find the ancient laws of the Hebrew people. The core of these laws are what we call the Ten Commandments. These commandments not only form the basis of most Hebrew laws, many of which are found in the rest of the Pentateuch, they also form the basis of common law in most of the Western world. The "Ten Commandments" were given to the Hebrews through Moses during their 40 long years in the desert.

Here's a quick summary of the Ten Commandments, in my words. I'd suggest you check them out yourself in the twentieth chapter of the book of Exodus (the second book in the Bible) and in a slightly different version in the fifth chapter of Deuteronomy (the fifth book in the Bible).

1. There is only one God. Don't go messing with any others.
2. Don't make "things" as if they were as important as God.
3. Don't trivialize God.
4. You need a day of rest. Make that day a special day to pay attention to your faith.
5. Respect your elders, especially your mom and your dad.
6. Don't kill.

7. Don't have sex with anyone except your life-partner.
8. Don't steal.
9. Don't tell lies.
10. Don't go wanting things that belong to somebody else.

Not a bad set of rules on which to base our lives! No wonder they became the foundation of the laws of most of the Western world.

Biblical Potboilers

The next part of the Hebrew Bible contains the historical books. This is far more recent stuff than the Pentateuch, and you can tell because it's full of delightful detail.

That detail includes an honesty not very common in folk histories. The heroes and villains of other cultures tend to be either absolute cads or superhumanly good, but the Hebrew leaders were totally human. There were no half-gods among them.

The stories, songs, and literature of Western civilization are full of images and ideas and sayings from the historical books of the Bible.

Hollywood has produced a bunch of potboilers based (usually pretty loosely) on these great stories.

My favorite among all the stories is about the greatest king of Israel, David. You've most likely heard the story of David and Goliath: how David clobbered the giant with a rock from his slingshot. It's one of those tales that probably got embroidered a fair bit in the telling.

David was, among other things, an exceptional leader and military strategist. He took Israel from being a two-bit principality into a mighty and respected kingdom. David was brilliant. And bloody.

He was also a passionate lover, and the story includes several accounts of his amorous adventures. The most famous concerns Bathsheba, whom David raped because, I think, he was in the middle of a midlife crisis. Then in an elaborate cover-up, David had Bathsheba's husband killed. The story doesn't whitewash the fact that the greatest king of Israel committed adultery and murder.

David had to pay dearly for his sins. But in spite of his wild passions and unbridled ambition, David was also a very religious person in frequent communication with God.

In David we can see the best and the worst of us. Those of us who have trouble keeping our lives on the rail recognize in David a kindred soul. My sins haven't been as colorful or dramatic as David's, but I find it comforting to read the story, because I figure if God loved David, maybe God can love me too.

Songs and Sayings

When David wasn't seducing women or fighting wars, he was composing songs. Tradition has it that David wrote some of the next section of the Bible known as the Wisdom Books.

The most famous Wisdom book is called the Psalms, which simply means "plucking of the harp." It's a songbook, and like any songbook, some of them are better than others, and everyone has their favorites. The psalms run the gamut of human emotions from the lowest

("My God, my God, why have you forsaken me?") to the highest ("Make a joyful noise to the Lord!").

The most famous Psalm of course is the 23rd. I remember memorizing it in school from the old King James Version of the Bible.

The Lord is my shepherd;
I shall not want.
He maketh me to lie down in green pastures:
he leadeth me beside the still waters.
He restoreth my soul:
he leadeth me in the paths of righteousness
for his name's sake.
Yea, though I walk through the valley
of the shadow of death,
I will fear no evil:
for thou art with me;
thy rod and thy staff
they comfort me.
Thou preparest a table before me in the
presence of mine enemies:
thou anointest my head with oil;
my cup runneth over.
Surely goodness and mercy shall follow me

all the days of my life:
and I will dwell in the house of the LORD
for ever.

Magnificent poetic language! If you love language well used, read that psalm (out loud if possible) and some of the other Psalms in the Jerusalem or New Revised Standard Version of the Bible. The poetry in the newer translations is not as traditional in style, but is every bit as magnificent as in the King James Version which some of us in the geriatric generation know so well. Let the images roll around in your mind and the sounds around on your tongue. A delightful experience.

One of the famous books in the Wisdom section is Job. Job isn't a book of history. Like the parables of Jesus, it's a story told to make a point. The story tries to deal theologically with the meaning of suffering. Why do bad things happen to good people? It's a gold mine of brilliant insight. From this book we get the phrase, "the patience of Job," though if you read the story you find that Job was anything but patient. You'll need patience to read Job though. Parts of it get pretty tedious.

The book of Proverbs has a bunch of delightful sayings, many of which you might recognize. So does the book of Ecclesiastes where you find the famous passage that begins, "To everything there is a season, and a time for every purpose under heaven."

For many years people were embarrassed about the Song of Songs (in some translations it is called the Song of Solomon), because it is frankly and beautifully erotic. Religious leaders went to great lengths (many of them still do) to prove that it was an "allegory." The argument doesn't hold water. Song of Songs is a hymn to the glory of one of God's great gifts to humans, the joy of sex. And that fact will only bother you if you think sex is dirty.

A Nonprophet Church?

The Wisdom literature is followed by the Prophets.

Prophets are a misunderstood bunch. Nowadays, the popular meaning of the word "prophet" seems to be more like "fortune-teller," someone who looks into the future to predict what's going to happen next week or next year.

The ancient Hebrew prophets (and there were a bunch of them) were never fortune-tellers. They didn't "predict the future." They were the religious, political, and social analysts and commentators of their day, a little like the editorial writers in the newspapers.

They looked around at what they saw, and found that much of it wasn't very pretty. They saw greed, the lust for power, and the rejection of God's love. The prophets called a spade a spade, and told people exactly what was going to happen if they didn't clean up their act.

People didn't like to hear that kind of prophecy then, and they don't now. In those days, the prophets got rocks thrown at them. They were killed and persecuted.

In the U.S., Canada, and most of Europe, religious prophets are mostly ignored. If a minister or priest speaks prophetically from the pulpit, the people are likely to look for another church. Or more often, start looking around for another minister.

Even today, prophecy can cost you your life. Archbishop Oscar Romero, a Latin American prophet, was shot and killed while worshiping in his own church. Martin Luther King, Jr., died for his convictions. Other modern prophets like Archbishop Desmond Tutu, in South Africa, risked their lives and the lives of their families to speak out against the evil of apartheid. I have a friend who works quietly trying to improve the lot of aging and sick seniors in the downtown core of the city. She is a prophet too.

My favorite biblical prophets are Isaiah and Jeremiah. Jeremiah had a great sense of the dramatic. He loved to act out his parables. Jeremiah went around smashing jars, cutting up scrolls and staging little audiovisual demonstrations to show what would happen to the King and his people if they didn't straighten up and fly right. He was slightly crazy, but God didn't seem to mind.

Isaiah is noted for his images of the "suffering servant," the idea that the nation of Israel should live its covenant with God, not by gaining power over people but by suffering and identifying with them. Christians have looked back at Isaiah's words and seen in them a description of the Messiah.

Certainly, Isaiah helped us understand that the greatest redeeming and loving strength comes through profound weakness. Isaiah would have had real problems relating to our contemporary "macho" power-driven culture.

And then there is the book of Jonah. It's quite a stretch to believe that Jonah was swallowed by a fish (not a whale) and then barfed up on the beach. Well, the person who wrote the story didn't believe it either. Jonah is a parable, not unlike the parables Jesus told to make a point. It is a piece of comic fiction told to convince the Hebrews that God loved and cared about everyone, not just the Hebrews.

I hope you got a good whiff of the delicacies inside this amazing collection called the Hebrew scripture or the Old Testament. Whether you read them for the literature, for the archaeology, or for the history, you'll find the Hebrew scriptures rich and delightful.

But why stand out on the doorstep sniffing, when you can go right inside the baker's shop? As one of the Psalms says, "taste and see that the Lord is good." Ah, that's the *pièce de résistance*.

The New Covenant

Christians read everything in the Hebrew scriptures in the light of what God shows us through the lives of people in the Christian scripture or New Testament. We read all the scriptures with the life and teaching of Jesus in our heads. That's why Christians and Jews have different interpretations of the Hebrew scriptures.

The Christian scriptures begin with three short biographies. Matthew, Mark, and Luke all contain versions of the life, death and resurrection of Jesus. You'll find many of the incidents and teachings in all three books. Some are told in only one. You really need to read all three to get a more or less complete picture.

These books are called Gospels, which simply mean "good news." Matthew, Mark, and Luke are called the "synoptic gospels" because they each provide a short synopsis of the story of Jesus.

The fourth gospel, the Gospel of John, is in a class by itself. It has lots of biography in it, but it's more of a theological study of Jesus, the Messiah. And John concentrates more on the resurrection of Jesus than any of the other books. Read John after you know your way around the basic story a bit.

The Acts of the Apostles tells the story of the first Christian churches. After the death and resurrection of Jesus, the disciples wandered around not really knowing what to do or how to do it, sort of a bedraggled "memorial society."

Then they shared a remarkable experience on the day of the Jewish feast of Pentecost, an experience that left them convinced that the

Spirit of God had come to them to give them power and direction.

We call the Pentecost event "the birthday of the Christian church." Things took off from that point, with all kinds of people joining the community.

Letters to New Churches

During the first years after the death and resurrection of Jesus, the authorities considered Christians a small—and pretty weird—sect. Plenty of people wanted to stomp on them hard.

One of those people was named Saul. But on the way to the city of Damascus to try to put a stop to this crazy sect, Saul had an experience that left him convinced Jesus was exactly who his followers claimed he was.

That experience changed Saul's life totally. He changed his name to Paul and became Christianity's most articulate missionary and interpreter. He traveled the whole area we now call the Middle East and southern

Europe, preaching and teaching and baptizing people. And Paul wrote letters.

Later, people collected many of those letters into the next section of the New Testament, called the Epistles. *Epistle* simply means "letter." Why we don't call them letters, I don't know. Like everyone else, Christians have a tendency to pick twenty-dollar words when a two-bit word would be clearer.

Paul was a scholar, a highly educated Jew who knew his way around the Hebrew scriptures. Because of that, Paul became Christianity's first "professional theologian." Even today, his letters to the young Christian churches in towns such as Rome and Corinth and Ephesus form the backbone of New Testament theology.

Personally, I find some of Paul's writing, such as the letter to the Romans, to be almost impenetrable prose. It makes me think Paul must have had two left feet. But when Paul writes to the Corinthians, some of his words dance right off the page.

Paul was writing to very real people, struggling to be Christian in some pretty tough circumstances. They had many problems, and they often messed up pretty badly. Paul didn't mince words when he wrote to them. Often when we read his letters, we wince because it sound as if he's writing to us, right now, in the twentieth century.

The End of the World

There are other letters in the New Testament written by various leaders in the early Christian church. And they are followed by the last and most misunderstood book in the Bible.

The book of Revelation was written at a time when the Roman Emperor was really putting the screws to the Christians. Christians were routinely being tortured and killed. Nero used to coat Christians with tar and set them on fire as torches for his garden parties.

A man named John wrote Revelation from exile on the island of Patmos. He filled his letter with rich images and metaphors and code words, all meant to encourage his fellow Christians who were having such a terrible time.

John wanted to help his persecuted friends feel that God was still in charge. Even though they were living through utter hell, John had a vision of hope on the other side.

Tragically, people often use the book of Revelation as a kind of religious fortune cookie. They try to crack it open so they can predict the future. They twist the rich images John intended for his hurting Christian friends, and they use them to predict the "return of Christ." These predictions would be funny if they were not so sad—even dangerous.

For one thing, focusing on predictions of the future provides a cheap way out for people who want to avoid the reality of the world we live in right now. People who focus their energies on predicting the "end times" don't have energy left to do much about the present. That gives them a neat way to escape Christ's call to "love your neighbor." Predicting the end of the world by quoting from the Bible is an escape from the heart of the gospel. Jesus warned people against that sort of thing.

Using the Bible to predict the future is very dangerous for another reason. Some people treat the conflicts described in Revelation as a prediction that nuclear war is inevitable. A few even go to the lengths of encouraging nuclear war because they think it's part of God's plan, which is utterly crazy and terribly dangerous.

As we approach the year 2000, I expect we'll see quite a rash of books predicting the end of the world. Don't buy them. You'll be able to get them at half price in the year 2001.

Using the scripture as a kind of crystal ball is a gross misuse of the Bible, and is definitely anti-Christian. I think it is downright evil.

A Rich Treasure

The Bible is a rich treasure of images and ideas and literature and metaphors. Any informed person should know the Bible because it has shaped our culture and our society more than any other document. It is still the world's best-seller.

Christians who read the scriptures through the eyes of faith find God in both the Old and the New Testament—God in the saga of a chosen people stumbling and struggling toward faithfulness—God in the life, the work, the teaching, the death, the resurrection and in the Holy Spirit of Jesus.

We see God acting in the struggles of the heroes and villains of the ancient Hebrew stories—in the enthusiasm and excesses of the world's first Christians.

We smile a bit wistfully as we read, because their struggles and their joys were not much different from our own.

We read, and we know God speaks to us.

—5—

About God

Remember the little girl who was going to draw a picture of God?

Like that little girl, almost everyone ever born has wondered, in one way or another, what God is like.

Christians are no exception. But we figure we have a head start because for us, Jesus was "God incarnate"—God shown to us in human form. So, unlike the little girl, we don't know what God *looks* like, but we're convinced we know what God *is* like.

What Is God Like?

The chapters on Jesus and the Bible should give you an inkling of the conclusions we've come to in the Christian church. But just so there's no confusion, I'll try to put these conclusions down in a few paragraphs. They won't do the subject justice. But then, this whole book doesn't do Christianity justice. No book ever will.

The first thing almost sounds obvious. There's only one God. Several thousand years ago that wasn't obvious because people tended to worship all sorts of different gods.

It isn't as obvious as it sounds today either. Your "god" is whatever you think is supremely important. For some people god might be a political system, or a philosophy, or music, or a lover, a new car or an expensive house. But for Christians, all those things, nice and important as they may be, are secondary. Only *God* can be our god.

Creator

There are three basic things we can say about our God.

God is a *Creator.* The Bible starts by telling us why God fashioned the world. Throughout the Bible, it becomes evident that God is still creating, most often creating new life in the hearts of women and men.

The Bible, especially that first chapter, tells us we've been given the world to look after. We're called to be cocreators with God, to keep on making this world a better and fairer place. We've been given the brains to look after it so that all human beings can live the way God wants them to live. So far, we haven't done such a hot job, not because we don't have the know-how, but because our priorities are cockeyed.

Redeemer

Second, God is our *Redeemer.* God loves us. Jesus told us about that when he used phrases like "life in all its fullness" to describe what God wanted for us.

The problem is that we're caught in a massive screwup. As individuals and as a society we keep making choices that get us into hot water. We rape the environment because we want to get rich fast, and then wonder why our rivers have become open sewers. We want to feel important, we want to have control, so we get it by walking over other people. We feel guilt and they feel anger, and before we get it sorted out, we're killing each other.

We want to feel safe so we buy guns and bombs. Those we see as enemies want to feel safe too, so they buy guns and bombs. Soon we're spending so much on guns and bombs that two-thirds of the world hasn't got enough to eat.

It's known as *sin*. Often when people think of sin, they think Christians are fussing about drinking and smoking and sex. Anything can be sinful if it hurts ourselves or others, but the big sins are greed, the lust for power, refusing to see our responsibility for what's happening in the world, and our failure to love.

These are private and personal sins and we each bear individual responsibility for them. They are also corporate sins, the sins of our town, our club, our church, the company we work for or own shares in, the government we elect. We are, each one of us, responsible for those sins too.

Some Christians feel there is a definite, identifiable evil force in the world. Some feel that evil takes the form of a "being" called the Devil. Others feel it is more of a dark force, a pulling away from God. Still others feel evil is simply the absence of God, that evil exists when we ignore the redeeming action of God.

That redeeming action of God is the life, the death, and the continuing presence of Jesus Christ. That action gave us all we need to get ourselves out of the personal, political, social, and economic mess we're in. Christians believe that a personal faith in the reality of Christ, plus a genuine effort to live out *all* the implications of that faith in everything we do, is our part in God's redemption, and our only hope for the future.

Sustainer

Third, God is our *Sustainer.* By that we mean something like a very good friend, someone you spend time with, someone you enjoy having around, someone you can talk to easily and naturally. A friend is also someone who is there when you need help or a shoulder to cry on, or even to get you out of hot water. We believe the spirit of God is just like that, a firm and reliable friend.

Friendships need work. You've got to spend time with your friends or you lose them. We spend time with God in prayer privately, and we do it together in worship with others in church.

But by using the word Sustainer for God, we mean more than a friend. We mean God who transforms us, compels us, changes us, drives us, inspires us, and gives us the courage and the love to go out and change the world.

A Three-headed God?

Here's a story that's a bit dumb, but it's fun. Old Herman Berkowitz had been hit by a car and was lying on the street close to death. A priest came by and asked, "Do you believe in God the Father, God the Son, and God the Holy Spirit?"

The old man rolled his eyes up into his head and said, "I'm dying and he asks me riddles!"

The priest was asking about the "Holy Trinity." The Trinity is an ancient concept that sounds a little crazy when you first hear it. God the Father, God the Son, and God the Holy Spirit. A three-headed God?

Yet the Trinity idea is a useful tool as we struggle to understand what God is like. Among other things, it means we experience God in three primary ways.

I spoke of God as the Creator a few paragraphs back. There are many other metaphors, words we use to talk about God who is "out there." The most common traditional metaphor is "Father," but there are many others such as "Judge," "Ruler," "Lord" and yes, "Mother." Jesus sometimes called God "Abba" which in his language meant "Daddy."

Remember the long list of names and concepts we had for God at the beginning of the book? There are hundreds more. None of them do justice to God, but all of them are useful. Some more than others.

Second, I spoke of God as Redeemer, or God as known through Jesus Christ, God as a human person. Here we're talking about the life of Jesus of Nazareth who was born and who lived and died at a particular moment in history, the Jesus we read about in the Bible.

Third, when I spoke of God as Sustainer or Friend, I was talking about the Holy Spirit: the God who is constantly with us whether we recognize it or not. We experience God as a personal presence with us in what is traditionally known as the Holy Spirit.

Of course, we experience God in more than three ways. And there are many other ways of talking about God. The reality of God is so vast, no human mind can comprehend it, and certainly no human words can contain it. So let's not get hung up on words. It doesn't matter what you call God. It does matter that you call God *something*, that you communicate with God.

God is out there directing the universe. God is also in the depths of the human soul. God is present, waiting, hoping, we'll take the plunge.

But I admit it sounds complicated sometimes, because we Christians often throw words around carelessly without thinking very much about what they really mean. Sometimes we talk as if Jesus Christ and God are the same (which in one sense they are), and then we talk as if they are different (which in one sense they are). We know perfectly well those ideas are contradictory, but they are somewhat clumsy attempts to grasp a reality that is too magnificent for our minds.

It gets worse. If you go to a Christian church service, you'll hear people saying, "God is spirit!" In the next breath, we'll talk about Jesus "sitting at the right hand of God," or that "God is seated on a heavenly throne." We know perfectly well that a spirit doesn't have hands, much less something to sit with.

It doesn't mean we're confused (though sometimes we are), but that we talk in analogies, metaphors and other poetic devices. The important things in life, such as love and truth and justice and hope can never be described in the precise language of science. Have you ever heard a love song that said, "My love for you is equal to 2,587 squared"?

We kiss, we hug, we give gifts, we have celebrations, we shoot off fireworks, we sing songs to express all those things which simply can't be confined to specific definitions. That's true in all of life. It is especially true of religion.

We Don't Know Everything

We have to use poetic words, symbolic acts, songs and stories to express our faith. We can't communicate without them. Sometimes we can't communicate with them either. They're slippery. Something that has deep meaning for you may not do a thing for me. And vice versa.

So you say I must be wrong and I say you must be wrong and, secretly, we both start wondering about ourselves. "She sees things differently than I do. There must be something wrong with me."

We have our doubts. Or at least we should. People who never have any doubts, who never wonder late at night whether they've got their minds all messed up around some medieval gobbledygook, are not doing much thinking about their religion.

Other folk are so insecure, they lock in on one particular perspective and defend that ferociously, refusing to admit, especially to themselves, that there might be another way of looking at truth.

Honest doubt is a gift of God that helps us sort through the garbage in our mental attics and throw out the junk that's no good any more. Some of the things I believed as a child served me well then. I don't need them any more. The only way I knew it was time to do some spiritual housecleaning was when doubts began creeping into my mind.

So yes, Christians have their doubts. We've got a lot to learn. We know that. If we didn't know that, we'd never make any progress. God keeps feeding us new insights as we struggle through our lives listening and praying. One of the ways God feeds us insights is in the middle of our doubts.

Struggling with those doubts, and enjoying the flashes of new insight as God is revealed to us in many different ways, through our study and work—that's one of the things that keeps the Christian life interesting.

—6—

The Church

When we wake up in the middle of the night, convinced that God is trying to tell us something, how do we know it's not the pepperoni pizza we had before bed?

We don't know. That's the problem. Over the centuries, we've discovered that the best thing to do is to take that new insight to the church. Not necessarily to our own little congregation, although that's a good place to start.

That way you can compare your revelation with the insight and perspective of the church through the ages and around the world. The church helps us sort out whether our "revelation" really was God, or an overactive imagination. That's one of the reasons we have a church. None of us is as smart as all of us. (I know. I'm repeating myself.)

When we speak of a church, we don't mean a building. Or at least, not primarily. We think of the church as God's people or God's family. We're called into the church community to worship God. That worship includes the prayers and liturgy and rites that we undertake there. But worship also includes the way we relate to other people and the way we live our lives.

What Is a Church?

There are several things most Christians believe about the church. All of them sound a little wild.

First of all, there's only one church. I know that sounds silly. Everybody knows there are several kinds of Catholics, a zillion kinds of Protestants, and a few species that haven't even been classified yet. Nevertheless.

Think of it this way. Bev and I are married, and so we speak of our various in-laws as "family." We have four kids, and we speak of them as our "family." When Bev and I lived in the Philippines, we got to know and love a young couple that we "adopted" as family according to an old custom of that country.

None of these people live in the same house, not even the same town with us. They all have their own lifestyle, their own way of doing things, even their own set of beliefs. There are some with whom we don't get along too well. Nevertheless, they are family. There is a reality to that concept, even if that reality exists mostly in our minds and hearts.

When the spirit of God came to those first disciples at Pentecost, it came to them in a strange and powerful way. Looking back on that event, Christians have realized that it represents the birthday of the church. It was the birthday of just one Christian church, not all sorts of different denominations.

But as the church spread out across the world, people developed different customs, different ideas, different styles of doing things. The cultures into which Christianity came contributed to the way in which the churches did things. There wasn't anything "right" or "wrong" about many of these customs.

For instance, at Christmas, when I grew up in the tiny town of Horndean, Manitoba, we always put out plates for Santa to put the gifts onto. When Bev and I got married and had kids, we borrowed a different custom from her folks: Christmas stockings. There's nothing right or wrong about plates or stockings. They're just customs. Traditions.

Each Christian denomination has its own customs and traditions. Sometimes these things cause disagreements. Seen positively however, differences can be part of our richness. Who wants a church or a society where all the ideas and traditions are put into one huge blender and everything comes out a dull gray sludge?

Furthermore, God doesn't necessarily say the same thing to every Christian. A person who is hurting and in grief may experience the loving, hugging arms of God helping them through their hurt. A sedentary Christian who is getting a bit self-centered may experience God as a swift kick in the backside.

Not only does God say different things to different people, we each hear God in a different way. People listen from their own viewpoint—from their own "mind-set."

For instance, Bev and I often go out for an evening, and then come back home and chat about the things we did or the things we heard others say. We often come away with quite different impressions.

"George was really upset about something," Bev might say.

"Really? He seemed extraordinarily cheerful," I reply.

"That's what I mean."

The Unpleasant Truth

But let's own up to the brutal facts. A big reason there are so many different denominations is because we've had our squabbles. More than squabbles. Fights. Wars in a few instances.

I'm not one bit proud of that part of Christian history. Critics of Christianity have used these divisions as an argument against Christianity, and they certainly have a point. On the other hand, political parties and democratic countries fight with each other too. Our democratically elected leaders have an interesting habit of talking like saints and acting like crooks. That doesn't mean there's no value in the democracy.

Democratic governments and Christian churches have this in common. The only leaders we can choose are human. If it weren't for people, everything would be perfect.

The other side of the truth is that our most humanitarian laws and concepts, most of our educational and medical systems—in fact so much of what is good and beautiful in our culture and society—have their roots in the Christian religion.

Of course Christians don't agree on everything. Disagreement can generate some very creative thinking. It can also generate a few bashed heads.

A prayer you'll hear said in churches of most denominations is a prayer asking God to forgive us for our divisions. Those divisions are a sin. They're something we're very ashamed of. But family quarrels are far easier to get into than to get out of. And many of these quarrels go back hundreds and hundreds of years.

However, we still think of ourselves as one church. It's only an ideal. But it's there in our thinking far more than most people outside the Christian family know or believe. The various Christian churches worship and work together more now than they ever have in the past.

Things are a lot better than they were. In almost every country there is a council or federation of churches, where the various denominations get together to talk to each other and to undertake joint projects. And just as a practical example, the first edition of this book was jointly published by Novalis which has a strong Roman Catholic tradition, and Wood Lake Books which has its roots in Protestantism. A few years ago, that wouldn't have been possible.

Communication between Christian denominations is better now than it's ever been, but we've still got a long way to go.

A Universal Church

We call ourselves a *catholic* church. The word "catholic" means universal. We believe the church includes all Christians of all time, including those who have already died, and those who will be born in the future.

A number of churches use the word "catholic" in their name, such as the Roman Catholic Church or the Ukrainian Catholic Church. Most Christian churches, including Protestant churches, consider themselves small "c" catholic.

But Christian unity is still a dream. The dream isn't helped much by a variety of groups that refuse to believe any other denomination could possibly be part of God's family. Some of these sectarian groups claim that they, and they alone, have a hot line to heaven. Scratch the veneer of that certainty and you find people so insecure that the only way they can survive emotionally is by shouting their bravado. Or shouting down anyone who seems to disagree even slightly.

Holy Smoke, Batman!

The second thing about the church: it's holy. That does not mean Christians walk around with their eyes rolled up into their heads, the way they're pictured in cheap religious paintings. We're not a bunch of "Goody Two-Shoes."

On the other hand, the church is not a social club or a charitable organization or an educational foundation or a political pressure group, although there are similarities.

The spirit of God set up the Christian church, gave it a special function, and made it the instrument of God's covenant. The ancient Hebrews and modern Jews feel they are God's chosen people, chosen to show the world what God is like and to act out God's will in their lives. Christians feel Jesus renewed and enriched that covenant in the Christian church, and created it to be the community of those who commit their lives to God.

Christians (including clergy) get no special privileges from God. No special treatment. No immunity from problems and pain. As Christians we're no smarter and no better than others. No less likely to mess up our lives. But we have been given a special commission. We have been chosen for a holy task—to act out God's love in our lives. Furthermore, we have special resources to draw on when bad things happen.

One more thing about the church. It's apostolic. That means we have a genealogy. We know where we came from. The first church leaders (called "apostles") were commissioned by Christ. Any strength we have as ordinary Christians, or as leaders within the church, was given to us by Christ through the apostles, and handed down through the generations of the church.

Different denominations interpret this in a variety of ways, but all of them affirm the general principle. That's what we're talking about when we use the term "apostolic succession" (another bit of jargon you can use to impress people).

Varieties of Ministry

Okay, so if the church was commissioned by Christ, what was it commissioned to do?

Ministry. That's another one of those "in" words that can mean nothing and everything, which is why it is both useful and confusing. By ministry, we mean the small corner of God's creation where we are asked to do our bit for our fellow humans. We're asked to do what Jesus would do for them, if he were in our place.

Jean Vanier, who has devoted his life to working with mentally handicapped people, speaks with great passion about the way the most severely handicapped people minister wordlessly to him with their eyes.

The data entry person, hacking away for seemingly endless hours, but doing that job as well as possible and trying at the same time to show kindness and caring to the others in the office, is performing a ministry.

A ministry is whatever God calls you to do, from President to ragpicker. Your ministry may be part of your job, or your job may be something you simply put up with in order to do your ministry. I have a friend who says, "I wait on tables so that I get to do my ministry." I'm not sure if that means the waiting on tables is the ministry or the ministry happens after work. Probably both.

Ministry is living and working with a sense of being connected to the love of God, and also connected to the community of God's people. Ministry is people working with God to be part of the world's answer, rather than part of the world's problem.

In other words, when we are baptized, God calls every one of us to a ministry. Not everyone hears that call, and some of those who hear don't respond. Some of those who respond are not very consistent in their ministry. But ministry happens when the people of the church live their lives with an openness to what God is saying to them.

The word "ministry" gets particularly confusing when we talk about clergy as "ministers." Clergy are not any more in ministry than any other Christian. But they are in a special kind of ministry.

The Same Ministry

God calls some people to go into full-time Christian service. That doesn't necessarily make them clergy.

For instance, I consider myself in full-time Christian service as a storyteller and writer. I'm not an ordained minister. I'm a layperson.

In the church, we have clergy and laypeople. Both are called to ministry, though not to the same ministry. One is not necessarily more educated, or more clever—not even more religious than the other. We simply have different callings, a different sense of what God would like us to do and be.

Clergy are most often employed by a church (though there are lots of exceptions to this), and most of their work is done within the church organization. Laypeople carry out their ministry where they work and live. In the church, laypeople are usually volunteers. A sad old joke in the church goes: "Clergy are paid to be good. Laypeople are good for nothing."

Ordained people are called to a special kind of ministry: the "ministry of word and sacrament." They are specially "set apart." Clergy are called to serve the church in ways other Christians can't. Clergy perform the sacraments and in various ways are the spiritual leaders of the church. They are called to a "vocation," which is something very different than a "job." The vocation of priesthood—to be "special agents" for God—is to serve in ways that are absolutely necessary to the life of the church.

I like to think of clergy as midwives.

Clergy are there to help people in their communities give birth to the God-given creative potential within them. They support us through the pain of labor, help us when there are complications, and celebrate the new life with us.

Depending on the tradition, these clergy are called ordained ministers, pastors, or priests. They are often addressed as Reverend or Father, but those titles have mostly to do with custom and courtesy.

Clergy have various functions, but they're usually spoken of in three categories: priestly, pastoral, and prophetic.

The Pastor

While leading in worship is certainly central to the work of the clergy, the pastoral function is just as central. In fact, clergy are often addressed as "Pastor" in many traditions. As pastors, the clergy use their spiritual gifts and their professional training to help people live their lives more fully, to respond more creatively to the love of their family and friends and to the love of God.

When pain and tragedy and sickness and death and divorce and anger happen, as they happen in every life at some time or another, the pastor tries to provide the spiritual help needed to get us through to the other side.

Of course, clergy aren't the only ones who do this pastoral work. Every Christian is called on to minister to others, to be friend and counselor and support. For clergy though, it is usually a full-time vocation for which they receive special training.

The Prophet

The prophetic role is something we all share as Christians, and in fact, sometimes laypeople are in a better position to be prophetic than clergy. I talked about this a little earlier when I was describing the prophets in the Bible.

Prophecy is not fortune-telling or predicting the future. Prophecy is standing up on your hind legs and speaking out when you see something rotten happening that's hurting people.

As a way of getting at the nature of prophecy, let's look at the major institutions in our society.

A few years ago I heard politics defined as "the art of the possible." With opinion polls playing such a large part in political decisions, you might also define politics as "the practice of whatever is popular." You could define business as the art of making money, and law as the enforcement of whatever is legal (though not necessarily just). Our media have, to a large extent, turned news reporting into a ratings game. News is whatever gets people to watch or listen or read.

Granted, there are many fine people in all these institutions, doing their darndest to make things more fair, more honest, more just. But the institutions as such, don't have justice at the top of their priority list.

Only the Church Asks

The church is really the only institution that has, as one of its top priorities, doing justice. The church is the only institution determined to ask questions such as, "Is it right?" "Is it fair?" "Is it just?" "Is it loving?"

Not all Christians ask those questions, though they should. And even the church as an institution doesn't always ask them very well or effectively. And when it does, the various parts of the church don't necessarily agree on the answers. But the question is there, at the top of the list.

The tradition goes back a long way. Thousands of years ago, a Hebrew prophet said it this way:

"What does God require of you, but to do justice, to love kindness, and to walk humbly with your God."

That concern for justice and truth, for what is good and kind and fulfilling for all God's people, including ourselves, is the content of our worship.

Pulpit Pounding Parsons

Worship is the major function of the church. Worship is the central act of the Christian community. Worship means far more to us than most people outside the church can imagine.

Part of worship has to do with community—Christians getting together to lean on each other, to encourage each other, to enjoy each other's company or to have fun together. "Where two or three are gathered together in my name, I am there with you," Jesus said to us. So Jesus is part of that community, whether we are praying or playing.

Christian worship is not the expression of a frightened bunch of emotional infants trying to flatter an egotistical god into doing what they want—though in some aberrations of Christianity it gets pretty close to that.

Christian worship is consciously spending time with God. We may do that alone in our private prayers and meditations. We may do that together in our Christian community. When we worship, we say thanks to God, we express our love, and we talk to God about the many things that concern us. We ask for help for ourselves and others. And sometimes we just listen, to see what God has to say to us. Sometimes we listen to another person. Sometimes we listen to the silence.

And we do all that through songs, prayers, symbolic acts, and by listening for the word of God through the liturgy, through the scripture, or through the preacher.

The preacher, in the Christian tradition, is not someone who makes a speech every Sunday, but someone who becomes a vehicle for what God is trying to get across to us. The preacher, preparing a sermon or homily, is doing something radically different from the politician preparing a speech for the Rotary Club. The politician asks, "What do I want to say to these people?" The preacher asks, "What does God want to say to them?"

Some preachers become very well known for their fine, moving sermons. They not only have carefully and prayerfully prepared for their sermon, they also use the best techniques of the theater to deliver the message with excitement and style. That kind of sermon is a rare treat.

Some parishes and denominations have built up a following around the colorful speaking style of strong preachers. They sometimes become more of a personality cult than a church. And when the personality is no longer there, for whatever reason, the whole organization collapses.

The sermon is one part of the fabric of the whole worship service, which includes prayer, the readings from the scriptures, singing, the giving of offerings. And all of that happens in the context of the whole life and work and ministry of the worshiping people.

Unfortunately, the word "preaching" sometimes implies some high and mighty, self-righteous prig raking us over the coals at great length, while we wallow in our guilt. No doubt some clergy have preached that way, which may be why the word "preach" has taken on that flavor. But they are the exception, at least in the churches I've gone to.

The Central Sacrament

Holy Communion, which is also called the Lord's Supper or the Eucharist, is central to the worship life of most Christian denominations. I'm going to use the word Eucharist, because that term is understood in all denominations, even when it isn't commonly used.

But first, I want to take a crack at explaining what a sacrament is. Like many other things we do and believe, the sacraments must be experienced to have any real meaning. There are a number of different sacraments in the Christian tradition.

In one sense, a sacrament is a symbolic action. It relies on the symbolic because there simply isn't any way to put the reality of the sacrament into words that would mean anything. Christians tend to talk about "an outward sign of an inner reality." It's a little like giving someone a gift as a way of saying, "I love you" when you know the words simply can't convey the whole meaning of how you feel. That's part, but not all of it. Not by a long shot.

A sacrament is also an action. The Eucharist is something we do together. It isn't something we attend. There are no spectators. It is the Christian community sharing a symbolic meal.

The Eucharist has its origins in the ancient Jewish feast of the Passover, the feast that celebrates the liberation of the people of Israel from slavery. That's the feast Jesus and his disciples were celebrating just before he was executed, in what we would call the first Christian Eucharist.

"Do this in remembrance of me," Jesus said, as he gave the bread and the wine to his disciples. And Christians have been doing just that remembering for 2,000 years. And the history of this sacrament, way back to the Hebrew slaves in Egypt, through Jesus' last supper with his friends, makes this for us a feast of remembrance, a feast of liberation from slavery, a feast celebrating the victory of life over death.

Every time we gather for the Eucharist, we commemorate this history. We not only re-member Jesus, but in a very special and par-ticular way we become part of him—or he becomes part of us. So we are part of his death and his resurrection, part of his ministry and part of his special community, the church.

We are fed—nourished—as we receive the eucharistic meal. Christ becomes real to us, present to us, a strength to us. That's why we never get tired of this seemingly simple act.

Personally, the Eucharist means different things at different times to me. Sometimes, it seems to be a nice, warm celebration of the community we share in the church. At other times, I feel deeply guilty and at the same time completely loved and forgiven, and profoundly thankful.

Sometimes at the Eucharist, I simply know that I am deeply in touch with the holy, the mysterious, the eternal. And that's an experience I won't even try to put into words.

Denominational Variations

Because the Eucharist is so crucial to who we are and what we believe, different denominations have some specific things they feel are critical to the celebration of this central rite. There really isn't the space to go into that here.

If you are interested in what a specific denomination does in this regard, check with a well-informed layperson from that denomination. Or talk to one of the clergy. For goodness' sake, don't accept as truth what you read in the popular press or see in the movies or on TV without checking it out. There's an excellent series of books, each of them about a different denomination, listed at the back of this book that will help answer these kinds of questions for you.

The Eucharist is very hard for those outside the Christian tradition to understand. Even those inside often have trouble with it. A fine friend, a Christian lawyer, read a draft of this book and described the last few paragraphs as "b.s." "There's something dreadful about 'This is my blood.' It's gory, barbaric, primitive. I can love a person without eating him."

I have no answer for that. I can only respond from my own experience. When I receive the Eucharist, I feel as if Jesus is calling on me to take his life into myself, and to live it for him.

Baptism

Baptism is another sacrament central to the Christian faith. It is a symbol of ending our old way of life and committing ourselves to a new way. It is the way in which we welcome people into the Christian family, and that includes the whole Christian family, not just one denomination.

The first Christians baptized adults by "immersion," by dipping them down under the water. Now, some denominations carry on that tradition, while others pour water on the head of the person being baptized, or sprinkle a few drops. The important thing of course is the depth of conviction in the heart of the person being baptized.

Some denominations insist that only adults, who can make up their own minds about their faith, can choose baptism. Other denominations also affirm the baptism of small children and babies, and in that case, the parents make the promises on behalf of the child, until the child is able to confirm those vows on its own. Infant baptism is done by sprinkling water on the child's head, or by making the sign of the cross on its forehead with water. Or both.

Eucharist and Baptism are the only two sacraments in most Protestant traditions. Other denominations have designated other rites as sacraments. For instance, there are seven sacraments in the Roman Catholic Church. In addition to Baptism and Communion, Roman Catholics celebrate Confirmation, when children make their own vows to confirm those taken by their parents on their behalf at Baptism; Penance, which is popularly known as "confession"; Holy Orders, for the ordination of clergy; Marriage, which of course is two people committing themselves to each other for life; and the Anointing of the Sick. All of those rites are celebrated by almost all denominations in one form or another, though they may not be called sacraments.

Some churches, such as the Roman Catholic, Anglican, and Lutheran churches tend to put a higher emphasis on the sacramental aspects of worship. Other denominations such as United Methodist, Presbyterian, Reformed, and Baptist churches, place a higher emphasis on the preaching and teaching aspects of worship.

Squeaky Clean Christians

With the new spirit of friendship among the churches, we're learning all sorts of things from each other. So in recent years, the more sacramental churches are putting a strong em-

"Stay Out of Politics!"

The complete Christian life means getting involved with other people. For starters, we get involved with the church community, where we go for love and for strength, for healing and for instruction. Then, we gather up the courage and the love and the insight we've been given, and go out there into the rest of the world to try to make it better, to struggle against the forces of death.

That's the point where the Christian church often gets criticized. "The church should stay out of politics and business," people sometimes say.

Well, we can't.

At least, not if we are going to keep on being Christians. In the first place, the Bible, and especially Christ's teachings, are full of statements and rules and stories and wisdom about business and politics and sex and that sort of "worldly" stuff. Jesus never asked us to be "pie-in-the-sky-by-and-by" kind of people. Jesus said that whatever we do for one of "the least of these" (the poorest and most helpless people) we do it for him.

It's very hard to get involved in the life of the poor and the dispossessed without getting mucked up in business and politics. Christianity is not a cream puffs on Sunday kind of religion.

As Archbishop Helder Camera said, "When I gathered food for the poor, they called me a saint. When I asked, 'Why are they hungry?' they called me a communist."

That's why the churches have been putting an emphasis on discipleship, on a strong, deep inner commitment to the gospel of Christ. It's not an easy commitment to make.

The alternative? Well, I can't talk about this without sounding as if I'm trying to twist your arm. But you've got me pegged by now anyway, so I might as well go for it.

The alternative to a life of faith, from my point of view at least, is half a life. You miss half the fun. And half the pain. But both the pain and the fun are part of the richness of it all.

In a sense, the beer commercial is right. "You only go around this life once, so you've got to grab all the gusto you can get." Except that you won't find much genuine gusto in a pub drinking beer. But if you try, you may find real gusto in the Christian church.

No, you won't find much "gusto" if you go at it reluctantly, popping into church every couple of weeks. That sort of nibbling at the Christian faith may do more harm than good if it inoculates you against the real thing.

Being a Christian is a little like being pregnant. You can't be "a little bit pregnant." But if you're prepared to make a full commitment, you'll find yourself birthing new possibilities, discovering new potential, and most of all, a brand new life.

If you don't like that metaphor, here's another one. You can stick your toe in the water once in a while, but if you want to know what the ocean of God's love is really like, take the plunge! Get wet all over. It may feel a bit brisk at first. But once you're all the way in, the water's marvelous!

— Postscript —

Is It True?

On a rock face, not far from our house, somebody has spray-painted "Jesus Saves!" in huge, drippy letters.

Fluorescent orange!

I think it's tacky and simplistic. Its tasteless-ness drags Christianity down to the level of an underarm deodorant.

But Frederick Buechner, who writes mar-velous books, has seen the same kind of sign in his neighborhood. After reacting much the same way as I did, he had the smarts to go on and ask the question, "Is it true?"

Ouch! That hurts! I'd much rather be self-righteously indignant at the kind of simple-mindedness that sign communicates, than face the question, Is it true?

I came across Buechner's question in his book *The Hungering Dark,* after I'd written the first draft of my book. I thought I'd brought the whole thing to a nice conclusion with an appropriate little flourish. Then I went on vacation. Through two weeks of glorious sunshine on Canada's west coast, I had Fred Buechner in my head pointing to that drippy spray-painted statement.

I finally decided I simply had to come clean. I've tried as hard as I could to describe the Christian faith for you without doing any convincing. Now it's time to let you know my bottom line.

I'd prefer not to react to an oversimplified statement like "Jesus Saves," but I have to, because that's the way Christianity tends to come to us through the media.

The first Christians, almost two thousand years ago, had a creed that was just as simplistic. The only thing you had to say to be considered a Christian was "Jesus is Lord."

There was a difference though.

To spray "Jesus Saves" in four-foot letters on a cliff costs $9.95 for a can of paint. To say "Jesus is Lord" in the early days of the Christian church could cost you your life.

The spray-painted sign reminds me of the romantic young jock who wrote to his girl, "I'd climb the highest mountain for your love. I'd swim the deepest river to be at your side. I'd fight the armies of the world to win your love. P.S. I'll see you Friday if it doesn't rain."

Words can be pretty cheap. Christians stand guilty of using too many cheap words and meaning too little by them. When we say "Jesus Saves," it begs a whole bunch of questions such as, Who is this person Jesus anyway? And what does he save? From what?

I read somewhere that someone had put a "Jesus Saves" sign beside a food store. The food store owner put up another sign. "Easy Mart saves you more!"

But I'm still avoiding the question. Is it true that Jesus Saves? Fred Buechner would really like to know. I would like to know. Shawna and Gary, the couple I introduced at the beginning of the book, would like to know. If you managed to get this far in the book, you probably would like to know too.

Shawna and Gary began going to church partly in reaction to the consumer culture that surrounds them. "The message seems to be, 'buy more, eat more, consume more,'" Shawna complains. "The only happiness offered me, as a woman, is to become Miss Perfect Consumer. And frankly, it scares the hell out of me."

"And happiness for the male," Gary adds, "is to drink the right beer, drive the right car, and become Mr. Perfect Consumer whose goal in life is to make a pile of money and seduce Miss Perfect Consumer. Not love her. Just seduce her."

I heard a sermon recently. The minister was expressing a fear that we're destroying the world we love. "We love the forests and streams. We claim to honor and respect all people everywhere. But we put our money and our energy into building more and more sophisticated armaments, while our forests, our streams and our people die."

The Roman god Saturn ate five of his six children. He would have eaten the sixth too, but his wife Rhea hid the last one.

Saturn was the ultimate consumer.

So does the Christian God have a better answer than the Roman god? Is "Jesus Saves" any kind of a response to the despair expressed by Gary and Shawna and that preacher?

Yes. For whatever that's worth to you.

I squirm when I see it in those bald, simplistic terms, because so often those little religious phrases become nothing more than good luck charms. They're used like magic incantations. If you say them at the right times, or often enough, they'll bring you good luck.

Phrases such as "Jesus! Jesus! Jesus!" and "Yes, Lord!" and "Praise the Lord" are used like mantras by some groups and as seductive slogans by TV evangelists. If you say them over and over and over they help you shut out the world, shut out reality. An escape. An addiction. A fix. They become part of the problem, not part of the solution. Maybe that's what Karl Marx had in mind when he said, "Religion is the opium of the people."

The problem isn't the words. The problem is their abuse.

In that sense, no.

"Jesus Saves" is no solution to anything if you mean that Jesus is a ghostly superman with a beard who comes flying in to save the good guys and zap the bad guys and make everything nice for those who flatter him the most or say the right words often enough.

But yes.

If we struggle to be faithful to who Jesus was and what he taught:

- by living ourselves into the love that Jesus showed us, the genuine, active love for all our fellow humans and for our world . . .

- by struggling hard and long and painfully to know the will of God as Jesus lived it for us . . .

- by being willing to pay the price of living out God's love, even when it means confronting the structures that are destroying us . . .

- by receiving the gift of deep joy and profound hope which this faith offers us . . .

If we're willing to live our faith in that way, then yes, I believe it is true.

Jesus saves!

Jim has also written what I think is a most helpful book for those grieving the loss of a loved one, a job, a marriage. . . . The book is *Surviving Death*.

One of my favorite writers is Frederick Buechner, whom I mentioned in my Post-script. The book I was referring to is called *The Hungering Dark*. Buechner has written many books and all of them are well worth reading.

Many clergy and other church leaders are "bookaholics," and tend to have personal libraries they don't mind lending to people who are genuinely interested in reading.

If you have no church connection, phone and make an appointment to talk with one or two clergy. Some of them are cranky and there are a few stuffed shirts, but the vast majority are personable human beings who will be happy to talk with you and respond to any questions you might have. But don't expect all of them to agree with everything I've said in this book.

If this book has whetted your appetite and made you want to explore further and ask some even tougher questions, then I am satisfied.

R.M.